WE SAY #NEVERAGAIN

WE SAY #NEVER AGAIN

REPORTING BY THE
PARKLAND STUDENT JOURNALISTS

EDITED BY MSD TEACHERS
MELISSA FALKOWSKI AND ERIC GARNER

CROWN ♔ NEW YORK

We would like to dedicate this book to the seventeen victims of the February 14 tragedy at Marjory Stoneman Douglas High School: Alyssa Alhadeff, Martin Duque Anguiano, Nicholas Dworet, Jaime Guttenberg, Luke Hoyer, Cara Loughran, Gina Montalto, Joaquin Oliver, Alaina Petty, Meadow Pollack, Helena Ramsay, Alex Schachter, Carmen Schentrup, Peter Wang, Scott Beigel, Aaron Feis, and Chris Hixon.

We would also like to thank the Parkland community and all the organizations that have reached out to MSD for their endless support for the students at our school.

Finally, this book is dedicated to all the aspiring student journalists across the nation and around the world. Your voice is important and should never be lost in the sea of mass media. You are the future of the First Amendment.   —Parkland student journalists

———

To my husband, John, the love of my life, thank you for always being supportive of my many projects and aspirations. To my children, John Thomas and Evangeline, you are my world and I love you.   —M.F.

———

To my children, Emily, Ally, and Brandon, thank you for making me smile, and remember that there is always light in the darkness. And to my fellow TV teachers who were there for me, and supported me every step of the journey, thank you—I hope you realize how much it meant to have you all by my side.   —E.G.

CONTENTS

PART TWO: MSD STRONG

PART THREE: WHAT COMES NEXT

INTRODUCTION

THE EVENTS OF FEBRUARY 14

by Melissa Falkowski, MSD journalism teacher

February 14, 2018, started almost like any other normal Valentine's Day.

In my first two periods, my creative writing students wrote love advice columns and turned famous love poems into "hate" poems—an activity for the angsty anti–Valentine's Day students. The day was filled with candy, balloons, stuffed animals, flowers, and a general show of love for each other. In first period, Samantha Fuentes shared chocolate-covered strawberries from Kilwin's, where she had just started working. At the beginning of second period, we spent fifteen minutes outside for our monthly scheduled fire drill.

The rest of the day passed pretty uneventfully—lunch, study hall, and finally newspaper class. I worked with staffers and editors on our upcoming third-quarter issue of the newspaper and stories scheduled to post to our website. Class and the school day were almost over.

Then, at 2:21 p.m. the fire alarm sounds. The class stops what they're doing and looks to me for directions. It's not normal for the fire alarm to sound twice in one day, but not totally out of the question, especially if culinary is cooking.

"We gotta go, guys. Get your stuff," I tell them.

Some of them grumble, and some of them roll their eyes. We are annoyed and inconvenienced. Haven't we already done this today?

I grab my cell phone and my keys, grab my emergency folder, and stand at the door counting how many students leave the room—twenty-five total, the entire class listed on my fourth-period roster. I want to make sure that I have them all when I get to my assigned evacuation zone. I close my already locked door and turn left, heading the fifteen feet to the double doors that will take me to the outside hallway.

The outside stairwell is crowded. I see one of our campus security monitors. I ask her what's going on.

"Someone set off firecrackers in the 1200 building," she tells me.

"Okay. Idiots," I tell her as I roll my eyes.

I turn to two other teachers to tell them.

The campus monitor calls to me. "Go back. Code Red! Code Red!"

The other teachers and I call out to the students in the hallway and the stairwell to turn around and go back. I pivot and walk quickly back to my room. As I open my door, I hear an administrator's voice come over the intercom. "Code Red," he says.

I'm the first teacher back to my hallway. I'm holding the door open as students file in. I'm yelling to kids in the hallway, "Get inside! Right now! Go anywhere. It doesn't matter where you are supposed to be."

They look confused.

Colleagues are starting to return to their classrooms and open up. One of them calls down to me and asks what's going on.

"It's a Code Red!" I yell to her.

"Are you serious?" she asks.

"Yes!"

Two out-of-breath students appear on my side of the hallway. I tell them to come inside. Students at the other end of the hallway are filing into classrooms. I decide to close my door. I already feel like I've held it open for too long.

When I turn and close the door behind me, I see all my students huddled into a corner of the room. They are in the exact place we discussed a month ago after staff training about active shooter situations. I returned from the training and mapped out an area of the room that I could make invisible from the door's window by covering it halfway with paper.

I move into the corner, pull out the attendance roster from my emergency folder, and start calling names. In total I have nineteen students with me—two who are not mine, and seventeen of my newspaper students. I'm missing eight students. As I get to the names of missing students on the roster, I tell the other students to text them and find out where they are.

They are located quickly; they're in the classroom beneath us in a closet. All eight of them are together. When they reached the bottom of the stairwell, another teacher pulled them inside.

I write down the names of the two extra students with me. Their classroom is across campus. I find out later that as their class evacuated for the fire alarm, they were told to just run. Their building is directly across from the 1200 building. They heard shots, but they say nothing about it to me or my students at the time.

One of my students asks me, "Mrs. Falkowski, are you going to turn off the lights?"

I forgot to turn off the lights. "Of course," I tell her.

I get up, turn off the lights in my room, and walk into my adjacent computer lab and turn those off, too. For the few seconds when I'm in the computer lab, I almost lose my composure. I'm shaking, and I can feel the tears coming. I take a deep breath and go back to the corner in the larger room.

It's 2:28 p.m. One student is already in the closet. She went straight there when she arrived in the room. I text my husband.

"We are in a Code Red. I'm locked in my room. With kids. I'm okay and I love you."

I text my husband again.

"I don't know what's happening. It could be the drill they said they were going to do this semester. But I don't see why they would do it at 2:30."

Now we can hear helicopters and sirens. I google Marjory Stoneman Douglas High School. The first link says, "Shots Fired."

I make the decision to move everyone into the closet. I pull out a cart and some things that are taking up room. I call the students over a few at a time. I tell them just to bring themselves and their phones—no backpacks. Just people, not things. I grab my phone charger from behind my desk, and we close up the closet.

The lights are off. It's dark, hot, and crowded. We have to stand shoulder to shoulder for everyone to fit. A few students are crying in the back. I use my phone's flashlight to illuminate the closet. I'm telling the kids over and over that everything is okay. We are together and everything is going to be okay.

Students are reaching out to their families. Texting friends. Checking social media and trying to locate siblings. Students are telling me students are shot. It's all over Snapchat.

I start getting messages in my group chat with three of my friends in the English department. It's 2:31. One of them teaches on the third floor of the 1200 building.

"Shooter up in my floor," she texts us.

"Actual or drill?" another teacher texts.

"Seriously. Actual. My door window is blown out."

A few minutes later she tells us her arm was nicked. I tell my students what's happening.

My mom calls. My composure starts to come undone. I give her one-word answers and then tell her I have to go. I know I'd lose all credibility if I'm crying in this closet while reassuring students that everything is going to be okay.

Despite all evidence to the contrary, I still have not fully acknowledged that this is really happening. This has to be the drill. It's supposed to feel and sound real. That's what they told us would happen. Still, there's a nagging feeling that things are not right. Now we are well past dismissal time. Nothing interferes with dismissal.

Things are tense in the closet. I try to lighten the mood. I tell them it might be too soon to talk about this, but I think we are going to have to start all over on the next issue of the newspaper. For a brief moment, we laugh.

At about 3:45 p.m., we hear noises and voices in the hallway. We have the closet door cracked for air. I click it closed. We hear more noises. It sounds like keys opening the classroom door. It's silent in the closet. Everyone is holding their breath. Someone on the other side of the closet door calls out, "This is the police. Is anyone in here?"

A few seconds pass. No one answers.

I tell my students, "I'm going to tell them that we are in here. They have keys."

Someone calls out again. "This is the police. Is anyone in here?"

I pull slowly on the handle, opening the door a crack.

I whisper, "We're in here. We're in the closet."

"Come out slowly with your hands up," the voice answers.

I repeat the instructions to my students.

I open the door cautiously and emerge to three SWAT officers with weapons drawn.

One by one the students come out of the closet as the officers shout to them to keep their hands up. They have us sit in chairs in the middle of the room. I repeat every instruction to them and reassure them that they are okay.

The officers use my classroom as home base—emptying each classroom in the hallway into my room. As students and teachers enter, they are visibly shaken, and some break down into tears. All the faculty members work to calm the students in the room.

At 3:53, there are 162 students and six faculty members sitting on the floor of my classroom.

We're moved in a single-file line with our hands up to the school media center. Students are allowed to take bathroom breaks two at a time. I help the media specialist pass out water bottles to the students who look flushed. After a few minutes, we are taken out a side exit of the media center. We are told to stay in a single-file line with our hands up and follow the officers' directions. We are led downstairs and eventually past the 1200 building and across the street from the school. We still do not have an accurate picture of what has occurred.

We are finally reunited with the eight students who were separated from us.

At 4:23 p.m., Robert Schentrup, a former newspaper student, texts me. "Hey are you okay?" I tell him I'm okay and out of the school. An officer comes by asking if anyone witnessed anything. None of us had.

She directs us to start moving down the sidewalk. I tell everyone to stay together. My students are talking about who they have heard has been injured, including Carmen Schentrup. As we reach the northeast corner of the intersection, I watch a colleague on a stretcher as she is loaded into an ambulance. She has blood on her clothes.

We are told we are going to the Marriott, except officers send us walking east on Holmburg Road, in the opposite direction of the hotel. My dad texts me—CNN wants to interview me. My cousin's best friend works for the network. I tell my dad to give them my number.

As we walk down the street, students from my class are disappearing from around me. Some of their parents are on foot and found us walking; other students walk home as we pass their neighborhoods. I call my friend who teaches on the third floor. She's okay; the bullet grazed her arm. She tells me Scott Beigel is dead and two other people. She saw at least three bodies as she left her classroom.

We hang up. CNN calls as I'm still making my way down the street. I guard my words. I tell the anchor that the government failed us.

After my call with CNN, I have six students remaining. We wait together in the parking lot of Parkland City Hall for their parents to pick them up. I do another phone interview. I've already told my husband not to come get me. I've resolved to walk home.

It takes until 6:30 p.m. for the last parent to arrive. The streets around the school are closed to traffic, and the parents of 3,300 students are all trying to locate their children. The last parent offers me a ride into neighboring Coral Springs. She drives me as close to my development as she can get me, but roads around the school are closed, and I live next to the school. As I walk home, I call Robert. By now, I've heard his sister is injured. We talk for a few minutes. They haven't found Carmen yet. He thinks she's at a hospital. His other sister is okay. I tell him to call me later when he has heard from Carmen. We hang up.

I do another phone interview. In the background I can hear the anchor. They update the story—seventeen dead. I had no idea. In my mind, there were three. Seventeen is an unfathomable number. I finish the interview and collapse on my front porch in tears. It's been twelve hours since I left my house for work, and in that time my whole world has been shattered.

At 2:57 a.m. on February 15, Robert texts me. "Wanted to update you on my sister. She was killed in yesterday's shooting."

It took me an hour to muster up the courage to respond with my condolences. It felt empty. It was not enough. No words could return Carmen or offer comfort for the unspeakably violent way in which she lost her life.

It was clear that on February 15, we had awakened to a new reality, and nothing was ever going to be the same again.

GETTING TO WORK ON THE NEWSPAPER

by Melissa Falkowski, MSD journalism teacher

The day after the shooting, a candlelight vigil was held at Pine Trails Park. A cross or star was erected for each of the seventeen victims. Students and faculty came to honor them. The morning of the vigil, I texted my newspaper students: "Today I have to ask you to do something that will be incredibly difficult. There will be a candlelight vigil today and we need to cover it. We have a responsibility as journalists to tell the story of what happened and the stories of those who have passed and were injured. No one can tell their stories better than we can. So I am asking you that if you attend any events or memorials that you take pictures, even if it is with your phone, so we can document the events and emotions of what has happened. If you can do some interviews to get stories, that would also be helpful. If you are not comfortable, I understand. The vigil is at Pine Trails Park at 2:30. If anyone needs grief counseling, it's all day today and tomorrow at Pine Trails Park Amphitheater. Grief counselors are also at the Coral Springs Gymnasium and the Coral Springs Art Museum. I also want you to know that I love you all and I am here for you if you need me."

Not everyone was ready, but several of them set out to report on the events of the previous day and the vigil. Christy Ma and Nikhita Nookala wrote the first two stories for our website.

Several days later, I met with some of the staff and editors at the Coral Springs Barnes & Noble to plan our next set of stories and our next print issue of the newspaper. Rebecca Schneid was adamant that we would not give the shooter any additional notoriety by publishing his name in our stories. Initially, I thought that was an overly emotional decision that we would discuss later. However, I came to realize that the national media was going to publicize his name ad nauseam, in every story. Our newspaper had a unique opportunity to tell the school's story in our own way. In the end, I never brought it up again. I respected the editors' leadership and we followed their decision. Recently released evidence has shown that the shooter was seeking notoriety and fame. This has reaffirmed their editorial decision for me. As teenagers, they felt that giving him that fame was not responsible journalism, which is something I think the professional press ought to consider when they cover these types of stories.

Working on the memorial issue was difficult. I read each of

the profiles through many rounds of editing. It was emotionally draining to read and reread about the lives of the seventeen people we lost and what they meant to those closest to them. It was hard on the entire staff, and there were many moments when the students and I had to take breaks for our own emotional health. There was also a tremendous pressure to get it right. There is almost always some small error in what gets produced in our classroom environment, but this time that seemed unacceptable. We strived for perfection because anything less felt wrong. In the end, we felt proud of the issue and believed we had done something that was healing both for ourselves and for the community.

Following the memorial issue, we started planning our fourth and final publication of the school year, which would be titled Taking a Stand. I canceled it three times as we were working. I was tired and drained from working on the memorial issue and in general from the above-normal demands at school on my time and emotions. In the end, it was my husband who convinced me to move forward. Generally speaking, he is not a fan of all the extras that I take on at school, so for him to tell me that I had to do it weighed heavily on my final decision to go through with it. He felt it was important to allow the students to contribute to the conversation on gun control, especially since the entire nation was interested in both their opinions and their coverage of the issue. Ultimately, I felt it was our responsibility to weigh in on the discussions surrounding gun violence, and also to document school history beyond the memorial issue. Taking a Stand was split between activism and gun violence. It was finished very quickly and is something that I am proud of the students for accomplishing. It is well written and a fitting end to our tumultuous school year.

The strength of Marjory Stoneman Douglas High School's journalism programs prepared our student journalists to be at the forefront of the rallying cry #NeverAgain after the devastating tragedy at our school on February 14, 2018. These students were already adept at using their voices to call for change within their school and community. They used their training to speak out on TV, on social media, and in articles published nationally and globally. The nation has been impressed with their strength, poise, rational thinking, and compelling arguments. Many of these students were part of one of the school's various media programs—the newspaper, TV production, the yearbook, or the literary magazine.

Every high school in America needs a supported and thriving student-run newsroom. Scholastic journalism programs cultivate student voices and prepare them to become active participants in our democracy as adults. Journalism teaches students to question the world around them and evaluate the reliability of sources as they write about important issues in their community. Student journalists learn the value of exercising their First Amendment right to free speech within their school newsroom environment. Even for students who will not go on to work in journalism or media, these skills prepare them to be our country's engaged and informed voters of the future.

FINDING THE LIGHT

by Eric Garner, MSD broadcasting teacher

In my career, I have taught all levels of the socioeconomic ladder. I could easily say "kids are kids." And there is some truth to that. Relationships, teenage angst, cliques—they all exist in every high school I've taught at. But what made the Stoneman Douglas students (the teens accused of being "crisis actors" on social media) so different when they were faced with violence in their own school? I'd say their environment and training made them uniquely qualified to fearlessly take the lead.

The school I came from before Stoneman Douglas fronted a busy road in the northern end of Miami. The students were wonderful, but many of them had difficult home lives. Eighty-five percent came from single-parent homes. Some parents worked multiple jobs to survive, and others didn't—one still truly bothers me years later, an able-bodied mother who didn't believe women should work, so her son worked through the night to be the sole breadwinner for his mom and sister. Some students lived in cars or shelters, or wherever they could put their head down that night. Breakfast and lunch served at school could be the only meals they got that day. Then they went home to the stark realities of many inner cities. They faced random drive-by shootings, prostitutes who would hang out at night in front of the school until around 6:30 a.m. (I learned early on to never be too early), and at one point a serial rapist. When a cousin or a friend died, their face was ironed onto T-shirts, and their funerals were partially funded by passing the bucket from class to class. And even with all that, it was an amazing school. Dedicated, wonderful teachers and students, and an ever-changing administration that went there to learn what an inner-city school could be. When students walked in, the streets were left behind. We created a safe, nurturing environment. It was the magic of the school. Our high school graduation rates were off the charts for a school in an economically depressed environment, and the rate of students moving on to college compared to many suburban schools. It wasn't that the community wanted to be in that position financially. Almost everyone was hardworking, good people. It just was what it was.

Parkland, on the other hand, is not anything like the inner city. Parents are small-business owners, lawyers, doctors. College educated. College is the expected next step for all graduates. Landscaping is immaculate. When the school needed to raise money, it did easily. Safety was provided by the county sheriff's office, with a substation a couple of miles down one road from the school. It's a small town, formerly horse country, north of a big town, Fort Lauderdale. When I first came to Parkland, I was in culture shock. It was what you hear teachers complain about—a parking lot full of cars *much* nicer than their own. My last school had about fifty spots for seniors to park in. Stoneman Douglas has a senior parking lot and a junior parking lot that hold hundreds of cars. For the most part, the basics were not an issue. Students had food, shelter, clothing, and safety. And their sense of social belonging, from family to community structure, is much more stable and intact than their peers in the inner city. At Stoneman Douglas, students started their educational life with so many more advantages. Until that day.

On February 14, their belief that their world was a safe place was shattered. Every student, every teacher, tumbled. My inner-city students would endure another random shooting over the weekend and people would mourn. It was a ritual repeated all too frequently. But Parkland is a community that held coffee and tea fund-raisers for presidential candidates on the weekends. Violence didn't happen here—and the town was torn open. The incident struck students who were well rounded, who were accustomed to engaging with politicians whether at their own homes or at school, who were well traveled—so they were used to planes, and Uber, and hotels; in short, they were affluent. Almost all the things that a lower-income school community couldn't provide was available to them. I'm not saying these students-turned-activists come from mega-wealthy homes . . . just homes that provided a strong foundation, where they took safety for granted. As they lost that safety—in school, no less, where they had always felt safe—they became emboldened. Not being safe and secure was new, and fresh, and raw. So they found an outlet for their new emotional state—through their activism.

Unfortunately, there was still pain. The entire community was in pain. For many, it still is. It motivated us all to *do something*. I believe it's a driving force for the activists—to make something out of their pain and to find the light in their fear, anger, and darkness. My answer was to create and guide a documentary.

It's my job as a teacher to teach as many sides as possible. Show them how to research, let them discuss in an open forum—but ultimately the essays, the interviews, the documentary are their ideas. While I taught them to find their position and to be able to defend it, I also counseled them to be objective in their journalism. My students were living a duality throughout this entire affair—on the outside, activists, and on the inside, journalists.

Most of the key players you have seen in the media were, or are, in my television production class. The "crisis actors" trained here daily. Many I've known their entire high school lives. Some I've taken on trips across the country. So what's the secret inside scoop on them? My class was part of the activists' training—their ease and calm before the camera would be twisted into "crisis acting." But from my perspective: I worry. I've been called Dad many times. In the middle of the real heat, days into the media firestorm, I asked them if they had been sleeping and eating. I could see on TV they hadn't been. They are eloquent. They are camera savvy. Fearless. But they are also vulnerable. Handling the media attention while you are in the center of the story yourself is a lesson we don't cover in class. Constantly flying cross-country to appear on television shows while missing the last few minutes of a normal high school experience can take its toll. There are chapters here that talk about that toll, and about what it feels like to become an activist overnight.

So where do we go from here—to heal from another tragic event in America? My student journalists, who you will meet through this book, have learned how to be at the heart of a story and still cover it. To go beyond themselves to do what they can to document an event, while hopefully finding a path to their own healing, and the healing of the community. It seems trite to say that no one who was touched by this will be the same. But it is true. We will all carry this tattoo on our souls forever. And by telling their stories, by using their skills as journalists to find and defend their positions, they have a powerful tool in their quest to make school a safe place again.

PART ONE

Activism

PUSHED INTO THE SPOTLIGHT

by Delaney Tarr

To me, the worst thing anyone can say to hurt us is that we're "just doing this for fame." It doesn't feel good to be called an idiot, or a Nazi, or any number of offensive terms, but to be fame seeking on the back of tragedy is just so much worse. To be fame seeking is to be selfish, uncaring of the victims, uncaring of the cause. It means that they think we wanted this life, that we asked for it. That couldn't be further from the truth.

Every day, I long for the life I once lived, for our community to be whole again. To just be normal, to not have to live with the heavy weight of grief and the realization that our Eagles are dead.

Living after a tragedy is so much harder than many realize. It's a struggle to even get out of bed each day, much less face a crowd and maintain some level of composure. We often say we'd give up all of our notoriety in a minute if it meant this didn't have to happen, and it's the truth.

Because, honestly, being well-known is hardly enjoyable. It makes every part of our lives so much harder. The anonymity that comes with being a normal person is gone, now replaced with strangers asking for selfies and with constant fear. Fear that, one day, somebody who recognizes us won't be such a big fan. Someday, one of those many haters on the internet will be the person we run into. In that moment, we could be faced with hateful words—or something worse.

Of course, fear isn't the only thing we've been forced to experience since becoming public figures. Our entire lives have changed, from our careers as students to what we do for fun. It seems now that because we're seen as pundits, faces of an important cause, the fact that we're just regular teens is forgotten.

Things like social media, once ways of relieving stress, are now a new pressure that we must live up to. Tweeting and posting for fun is gone, as is getting to relax. Every move we make feels monitored, like the world is waiting for us to misstep. It's stressful, knowing that you can't act like a "stupid teenager" without being vilified. School is no longer a fun way to see your friends, but an impossible balance of work and education, fielding calls from reporters while trying to do an assignment.

It is not only our work that people care about; it is our personas. We have no freedom, no downtime, no chance to just be us. Rather, we are shuffled from one destination to the next, making rounds and saying the right things to help push our goals. We work down to the minute to organize and strategize what to do next, how best to mobilize the population. Our youth is gone, replaced with an endless cycle of responsibilities.

Of course, there are reprieves. With immense recognition comes a sort of privilege. Often, we are introduced to celebrities we've watched on our screens and onstage for years. A meeting with an idol can take some of the weight off, but only temporarily. Because when we get to meet those icons, we are forced to remember why we have the opportunity. These famous people are also looking to us to find a way to make a change that has seemed impossible for so long. We are forced to remember that they are only speaking to us because our peers are dead and we're doing something about it. Reminders like that, moments like that, they hit hard.

We're still grieving, and that's something people often forget. Amid the whirlwind of marches and press and television is a group of heartbroken kids. We barely took the time to recover, much less healthily process our emotions. Since day one, it has been a nonstop battle in a fight that we shouldn't be leading. But we are leading it, because circumstances forced us to step up. We've been propelled onto the national stage, where we are open to a level of criticism that no teenager should face. We are treated simultaneously like adults and children, neither respected nor understood.

But that just seems to be part of being an activist so close to the cause. Sure, this is a movement based in more than emotion, but the pain of loss is where it lies. The hurt and grief are why we go out there in front of the cameras every day. It fuels us to keep going even when we want nothing more than to hide away. It is exhausting; it is frightening. But it is also essential.

We do it anyway because despite how hard it may be to be a "celebrity," it's the right thing. We stepped up, we spoke out, not for fame but for friends. For family. The fight for gun control is so important to us that our personal lives are a worthy sacrifice, no matter how difficult it can be. Everything we give up, every luxury or part of us, simply makes the cause matter that much more.

That does make the victories more rewarding, though. There are moments when the celebrity status is beneficial. It's not in the special privilege, but in the way it can inspire those around us. The way it motivates people just like us to work hard and become activists in their own communities. Meeting someone like Halsey is cool, but meeting a little girl who is excited just to speak to you about her own activism means so much more. Connecting and reaching out directly to people in a way that only someone with hundreds of thousands of Twitter followers can do, that is what this movement is about.

This has never been for the celebrity. In fact, it's been the opposite. Not to seem distant and untouchable, but to seem real. To be genuine. To make true connections with our peers and inspire them to do their own work. Rather than celebrities, we are *examples*. We are proof that you can do it, too.

The Student Journalists of
Marjory Stoneman Douglas High School

NEWSEUM INSTITUTE NEWSEUM

SWEATING UNDER THE SPOTLIGHT
Recognition and Responsibility

by Nikhita Nookala

Historically, high school student journalists don't enjoy much freedom. They are occasionally controlled by the administration of their school, limited from public press areas unless specially invited, and generally taken a lot less seriously than an established press company.

Sometimes it is even difficult for a high school press group to gain recognition for their work from their peers. A common sight in our school in the days before the shooting was the stack of papers delivered to classrooms staying there unread for days, copies of the issue in the trash, or insert ads strewn all over campus.

After, though, everything changed. Hundreds of people were waiting to see what we put out. When Christy and I ran the first two articles following the shooting, covering the event itself and the vigil, more people commented on it than we had ever seen before. In the weeks following, Mrs. Falkowski had to upgrade the capacity of our website because it was getting more traffic than it could handle. This was something new for all of us. That was when we realized that the *Eagle Eye* had a loyal audience, and it wasn't just limited to the student body of MSD.

Suddenly, we were working with the *Guardian*. The *Washington Post* wanted to film us in our classroom. People wanted to make documentaries. *Time* wanted my friends' photographs. All these media outlets, which we never thought we would ever interact with, wanted to talk to us and write with us and listen to us. It was one of the most overwhelming things I remember about the aftermath of the shooting. Almost every day, we were doing interviews about press coverage or the shooting itself.

When we went to D.C. for the March For Our Lives, we experienced a whole different type of attention. We were treated like VIPs, given a tour of the Newseum, and offered the opportunity to cross over between the student section of the march and the press section. It was coverage that no one else would have the opportunity to experience, a perspective that no one else would have.

We were given the opportunity to talk about journalism and the work that we were doing on a panel that was televised. That was when it really hit me, that people were reading and watching and listening. Christy, Kevin, Emma, Rebecca, and I walked onstage, and before we had said a word, people were standing up for us. Us, five kids from Parkland who wrote for the school newspaper. For a few of us, our first trip to D.C. felt like being in a movie. People were asking us serious questions, people wanted to take photos with us, and every time, I felt like asking, "Why?"

Backstage at the march, Kevin and I got to interview people, who before would probably never have given us a second glance, by flashing my *Eagle Eye* press pass and saying frantically, "We're from the Stoneman Douglas newspaper!" It was a job that had to be done, but every second that we were doing it, we felt guilty. It was the deaths of seventeen people who went to our school that had taken us this far from home. It was tragedy that gave rise to the march itself.

I think every one of us would rather not be known for this. It was tough to balance being a journalist, a student, and a grieving friend. But it was up to us to not let those seventeen lives be lost in vain. We had the platform, so we were determined to use it.

We received a weird sort of respect from professional journalists. They were very nice to us for the most part, and offered their help and their media outlets to get our message out there, but we could never tell if they took us seriously. All we could do was make sure we put out our very best.

That was a lot of pressure. From being a publication that could get away with a couple of typos or design errors, we began our work on the memorial issue, which could *not* have mistakes. A mistake in the memorial issue was our worst-case scenario. When the *Sun Sentinel* was reprinting it, when the *Washington Post* was reprinting it, when thousands of people were going to read it, a mistake would cost more. While most journalists are used to this high-stakes environment and get paid to be in it, we weren't paid anything. We did it because it was our passion, and we had nothing to gain but the respect of our peers. That, in many ways, was much more valuable to us.

With power comes responsibility. Soon our newspaper and our staff were getting access to a lot more events because our perspective as the MSD student journalists had become valuable. We were able to cover stories that we usually couldn't because national events suddenly became connected to us. We were asked by every interviewer to criticize professional news coverage of our school, even though many of us were new to journalism.

One of the things that hit me the hardest about how our power had changed was our visibility on social media. While before February 14 I was tweeting links to our stories to add a few points to my grade, now those same tweets were being read and retweeted around the world. People from the UK, Australia, and Canada were commenting on our website, adding their thoughts about what was going on at our school, the same school that was nearly anonymous in our own country for years.

The way we embrace our gatekeeper role has also changed. We have the power to give a bigger platform to individual students and guests, and it is up to us to pick who should write about certain topics or be quoted in articles. Each decision is carefully weighed by those of us on the editorial board. We think about potential backlash, we anticipate the criticisms we will get with all options, and then we choose which criticism we can back up, because there will always be people who disagree with our final decision, no matter how much thought goes into it. Students who are respectful to other students and teachers will always be included to the best of our ability, regardless of their views.

I think this gatekeeper role has become the most draining of all.

Going back and forth about whether to publish a fourth-quarter issue, realizing that a trigger warning was needed to separate the gun-related stories from the other stories, trying to sift through the millions of gun-related facts to find the most relevant—all those things reminded us of how many people are watching. They reminded us that we still have to remember that MSD kids come first in our audience. They reminded us that we were there that day, too. We were so emotionally and physically tired that it was tempting to just give up.

But looking at what was going on every day, how many kids were standing up for what they believed in, even to the point of getting arrested, it reminded us that we needed to keep going, despite the criticism. We owed our school a complete record of this school year. In the future, people should remember that the *Eagle Eye* was always by the students and for the students, regardless of who was filming us or writing about us or calling us out. No matter who was watching, we needed to do what we knew best: report.

THE ROLE OF A JOURNALIST

Exposing the Epidemic of Gun Violence

by Rebecca Schneid

One of the first movies that exposed me to the world of journalism was *Spotlight*. I watched it on my computer when I was fourteen, and the narrative immediately captivated me. As a huge fan of movies, I have always looked for diversity in entertainment—movies that showed the different, and sometimes troubling, experiences of people in the world, and *Spotlight* was a perfect example. It depicted *Boston Globe* reporters who worked tirelessly to expose the Catholic Church's attempts to hide child-molesting priests from the public.

I remember thinking, "Yes! This is the kind of thing I want to do. I want to show the world the injustices they can't see. I want to make a difference like they did." Fast-forward to this past January in AP U.S. History class. We were learning about the Progressive Era of American history, where investigative journalists called muckrakers would rake up the dirt of American society and expose it to the world. One month later, I became intimately aware of a specific epidemic plaguing this country: gun violence.

When we began reporting about our school after the shooting, including the walkout and the march, it was our top priority to uphold the highest journalistic standards by remaining as impartial as possible. We felt a responsibility to report the facts of what happened at our school as we knew them from the inside, and to correct the public record that was so skewed by misinformation. As we did our work, we also discovered the power of the platform that we had.

The *Eagle Eye* was now in the spotlight, especially after our memorial issue came out. People were actually listening to us, both as survivors of a school shooting and as the newspaper of Marjory Stoneman Douglas High School. We realized we had a duty to discuss the epidemic that had left our community broken. We researched and researched and became knowledgeable about the statistics, causes, and laws surrounding gun violence.

As victims of this horrible massacre, we had a unique perspective on this issue, and it was important to present an insider's view of not just the facts about gun violence and its causes, but the impact on survivors—an ever-growing group. We also wanted to write about the laws addressing mental health, gun control, and school safety—what they currently are, what they've been in the past, and how they could change to prevent what happened to Stoneman Douglas from happening to another community.

Just as Upton Sinclair's *The Jungle* exposed the abuses of factory laborers and the gross reality of the meatpacking industry, we wanted to shed light on the truth about gun violence in this country. We wanted the world to see that even when the news cameras fade away, the trauma of gun violence remains in every place it tore through. Not only that, we wanted to share our spotlight with the hundreds of other communities across the nation that had to combat and live with gun violence on their streets every single day.

We used infographics, partnerships with larger newspapers, and public activism to demonstrate to the people watching that *this was not normal.* And that is a fact.

So from there we used our platform to raise the voices of our classmates, peers, and strangers alike, who all had a perspective on this issue. Conservative or liberal, it became clear that all in this nation want to see an end to this epidemic. (I call it an epidemic because gun violence kills ninety-six people every day.) And just like any epidemic, it can be cured. The issue is that each perspective seeks a different treatment. Some say that gun control is the only cure, while others advocate for school safety. We wanted to give advocates for each of these perspectives the opportunity to voice their concerns and opinions, while at the same time presenting the facts of the situation.

From the beginning, Mrs. Falkowski set an amazing example for us. She started speaking out on the day of the shooting, just as angry as the rest of us that this was able to happen at our school.

She took the lead, making sure we understood our role and responsibility as the reporters for our school newspaper. She pushed us toward excellence when writing and designing our memorial issue, our activism special issue called "Taking a Stand," and our online stories. Without her fierce leadership, we would never have had the courage to use our newspaper and our reporting to educate and influence others.

This happened to our school, and this was *our* story. So we wanted to be the ones to tell it. We raised the voices of our peers and exposed gun violence for what it truly is: a disease. The *Eagle Eye* will continue to be the voice for MSD High School as our activism continues.

EXTRAORDINARY ACTS

Senior Brandon Huff Tries to Run into Freshman Building to Save His Girlfriend

by Lauren Newman

On Valentine's Day 2018, senior Brandon Huff had planned for a romantic evening with his girlfriend, senior Jessica Luckman, but sadly their celebration never happened. Huff was outside the Marjory Stoneman Douglas cafeteria filling up his water bottle when the fire alarm went off. He proceeded to walk back toward his classroom to meet up with his classmates for the drill when his phone buzzed with several texts from Luckman: "baby there's a shooter in my room," "there's a gun," and finally "I love you." Luckman was in AP Human Geography teacher Ivy Schamis's fourth-period class on the first floor of the Freshman Building.

Huff immediately dropped his water bottle and hall pass and picked up his cell phone. Changing directions, he started running toward the 1200 building, talking to Luckman on the phone, with the intention of entering the building.

"All I could focus on was doing anything I could to get her out of there safely," Huff said. "When I tried to run into the Freshman Building, I wasn't thinking, I was just acting."

However, Huff would not reach the freshman halls. A police officer posted outside the building prevented him from entering, understanding the danger Huff would be putting himself in had he gone after the shooter. The officer guided Huff to the auditorium, where he and dozens of others hid for over an hour.

"What Brandon did was selfless," Luckman said. "Although stupid for trying to run into the building with nothing to defend himself, that wasn't what he was thinking about. He puts others before himself, and I'm the luckiest person in the world to have him. I love him for trying to help others and am beyond proud of him."

The two stayed on the phone until the SWAT team came to rescue Luckman and her class and she had to put her hands in the air. According to Huff, if he had successfully made it into the building with the active shooter, "I would have tried to get to my girlfriend's class to make sure she was okay and comfort her in any way I could have."

While Huff admits that his attempt to run into the building was rash, he says that his only regret is not making it inside. "Even if I wouldn't have stood a chance against the shooter, I would've done anything to try and save at least one life," Huff said.

The couple was reunited several hours later at Luckman's home. "It was a relief to see that he was okay with my own eyes,"

Luckman said. "It's still a shock that this is all real life, but it helps having each other."

While Huff was unsuccessful in his attempt to stop the shooter, his act of love and self-sacrifice for his beloved girlfriend manifested the true spirit of Valentine's Day.

GUIDE FROM A JOURNALIST ON THE OTHER SIDE

The Dos and Don'ts for Journalists Covering Tragedies

by Carly Novell

Within what seemed like minutes of this disaster, hundreds of reporters were begging me for quotes and interviews. As a fellow journalist, I wanted to take as many offers as I could, attempting to help people who needed a student voice for their stories. However, with some journalists aching to get a good quote or uncover the story of what happened, they forgot that they were talking to someone who had just gone through a traumatic event. While it's important to get the story out, it's also important to be courteous to the victims and their grief. Here are some dos and don'ts for journalists navigating their way around this.

DO make the interviewee feel comfortable. The best quotes are given when the person being interviewed feels comfortable enough to reveal and share. For one of my interviews, the reporter asked to come to my house. Obviously, I was nervous, as I usually am when someone comes to my house for the first time, especially a reporter I don't know. To my surprise, this reporter made sure I was as comfortable as I could be in terms of not only where and how I was sitting, but also the questions she asked, which were well written and easy to answer. This interview was a breath of fresh air in between the constant three-minute phone interviews from other journalists aching for a good quote.

DON'T ask "how did you feel?" questions. I had countless questions regarding how I felt when I was in the closet, or how I felt when I heard my school was getting shot up. During those moments, the last thing I was doing was analyzing and questioning my thoughts and feelings. These types of questions also pressure the interviewee into thinking they should feel a certain way. After the shooting, I felt totally numb. I understood what happened, and why it was sad, but I couldn't *feel* my sadness. I spent a lot of energy judging how I was feeling before I could even feel it. How am I supposed to know how I feel or how I felt? My school just went through a shooting, and it's not like I've experienced anything similar to this before. It is important that the journalist recognizes this—although "how do you feel?" questions are a reporter's go-to, for people recovering from trauma, it's more than just a question, it's a pressure.

DON'T pester the interviewee. As a journalist, I understand the importance of meeting deadlines, but reporters also have to understand that they are dealing with someone recovering from intense trauma. If the interviewee doesn't answer your text right away, don't keep calling them until they get so annoyed that they answer just to make you go away. It is easy for us to distinguish the genuine journalists from the story hunters, and we are worth more than a story.

DO be thought-provoking and creative. Ask questions that the interviewee might not have been asked before. Ask them questions that make them really think about the event, without putting them back into the trauma. A question such as "How do you see your senior year making a lasting impact on the rest of your life?" has much more significance than "Did you know the shooter?" Ask open questions for the interviewee. Get their opinion and quotes on relevant topics instead of twisting their words. Journalism surrounding school shootings tends to be formulaic—it's extremely important to make sure that the individual community stands out. The journalist should reveal what sets the community apart from others in a variety of ways. There are so many angles to take on different parts of a shooting and its aftermath that there is no excuse for writing a dull, repetitive story.

DON'T induce anxiety. One of the worst things a journalist can do is ask the interviewee the story and details of the traumatic event they witnessed. Asking a victim to relive their experience is like asking them to jump in front of a moving car just to give you a better story. Your job is not just about getting a story to your editor; it's not worth putting someone through more pain than they've already encountered to give your story more impact.

DO cover the feelings behind the trauma. Talk to witnesses—inside and outside the community. Find an angle that distinguishes your story from the rest. I saw hundreds of the same articles about my school, and at some points it made me lose hope in journalism. I ached for creativity and unique reporting, but I just kept seeing variations of "17 killed in school shooting in Parkland, Fla." Cover what surrounds the facts. Cover the feelings, and not just the surface ones. There is significant complex trauma in this community, which deserves to be publicized. The state of my country, and my school's shooting, as well as others', has left the next generation of adults feeling hopeless. Why plan for our future when it probably won't even exist because of gun violence? Cover *that* pain. This is more than us mourning for a week, complaining for a month, and finally disappearing. These are lives that are ruined. Journalists need to find a way to not only display the pain to their audiences, but to help them understand it in a more profound sense. The hundreds of stories covering the same topic without a unique angle hardly do this. Pictures of vigils were an insufficient exhibition of our grief.

DON'T focus on the shooter. While the shooter's goal is to kill people and ruin lives, he also craves the fame and attention that accompanies it. Plastering his face on every social media outlet and publication does nothing except strike fear and pain in the minds of those who experienced the event. The "No Notoriety" campaign asks others to refrain from sharing photos and videos of the shooter, or even saying his name. The shooter does not deserve more coverage than his victims. I do not want to remember his face or name; I want to see this not happen anymore.

DO commend those who have enacted change. So many indi-viduals and groups turned toward activism and became heroes in our community after the shooting. They effected change and impacted our generation. It's important to attribute the change to the ones who began it, but it's also important to recognize all those who have made change, not just the most vocal. It is a journalist's job to see how things changed, what changed, and who impacted that change on a local, regional, and national level.

DON'T forget Parkland or any other community forever changed by gun violence. We are more significant than a passing news headline. We are grieving, and our lives will never be the same. This is more than a story with a beginning and an end. There are thousands of stories from thousands of personal connections to a tragedy. Just because gun violence and shootings are common doesn't mean each event is any less significant than the last.

Photo by Lisa Mizen

AN OUTSIDER'S PERSPECTIVE

by Lewis Mizen

The 2017–18 school year marked my first year in Newspaper, a class I was taking following a year in TV Production. Once I realized that I had an ability to write even though I lacked the technical aspect of reporting on the news, I thought I should participate in the newspaper program. Mere weeks into the course, however, I wished I had joined the program in my earlier years at Stoneman Douglas, as I fell in love with writing for both online stories and print.

Working alongside my friends long after class had ended to get issues over the finish line was a fun learning experience. Dealing with deadline pressure was nothing new for us; any high school student will tell you that. But to create something as intricate and prominent as the school newspaper brought an extra incentive to finally get an issue done. My participation in Newspaper was not limited to the classroom. Instead, it allowed me to explore the school and the community, and gave me an appreciation for journalism and media that I had never had.

However, the personal background that I brought with me into the room quickly caused a cultural and a political clash. The cultural clash came about due to the fact that I was born in England, and as a result my writing reflected both English spelling and wording. I was commonly scolded for spelling words like *favorite, color,* and *center* as *favourite, colour,* and *centre.* Oh, and don't even get me started on AP style! In the beginning of the year, I attempted to decipher where all the so-called "problems" were in my writing, but after coming up short due to my belief in the superiority of my writing, I gave up and decided to leave that as a problem for the editors, quickly making me one of the most despised writers to edit. Another issue that came up, less of a cultural clash and more of a personal preference, was that my style is to write elaborately, with sentences that were three or four lines long. My tendency to write such lengthy diatribes, along with my refusal to break them into separate sentences, was even pointed out at the newspaper awards at the end of the year, where my plate read "Has the highest probability of writing approximately 1,000 long words in only one article with the entirely of the article written in a single sentence."

After the massacre at my school, my foreign status served both to my advantage and to my detriment. The advantages I found were the ability to see the situation from an outsider's perspective, to recognize the flaws in a society that I wasn't born into. I was able to promote the best parts of the society I had become a part of, while at the same time offering alternatives from a society I had once called my home. Gun control is an almost solely American issue, and being free from the relentless conflict that has permeated society on the western side of the Atlantic allowed me to come at the problem with only my experiences to stand by, not any prejudice or stereotype. However, there were disadvantages to being born on the east side of the Atlantic. Most notably the fact that whenever people would tell me that my vote could be the vote that helped fix the issue, I had to remind them that I could not in fact vote. I even mentioned my inability to vote in a short speech I gave to the junior class of a school here in South Florida when advocating for them to vote when they came of age. Despite my inability to vote, I truly believe that because I grew up in a society free of school shootings, my views of the issue are mine alone, and I can stand by them regardless of influence or outside pressure from those who would disagree with me.

The political clashes that I faced came about due to my political beliefs, and the tendency for the majority of the media to lean more liberal than conservative. Despite my liberal views on social issues, my conservative stances on economics and foreign affairs often led to me being called up to write the conservative side of opinion editorials. I quickly found a knack for editorials and ended up competing in the editorial category at the Florida Scholastic Press Association awards, writing a conservative stance on the kneeling controversy that was sweeping across the NFL. But I didn't appreciate the assumption in the newspaper classroom that I would always take the far right or Republican viewpoint for editorials. While I may have sided with the Republican beliefs for a number of editorials, being pigeonholed as a die-hard conservative on every issue was unfair and led to a number of people being predisposed to disliking me. In fact, I heard from a friend that many girls claimed that while they would have been interested in going out on a date with me, the mere fact that I was a Republican turned them away.

Things like that, dismissing someone based on their political affiliation, is a failing of today's society. The fact that I call myself a conservative or a Republican does not make me a racist, homophobic, gun-loving bigot. In fact, I am none of the above. Stereotypes based on my political affiliation are wrong, because my political beliefs don't define who I am; they simply define the way I believe the world should order its ideals.

However, my core values are not always represented by the elected leaders who are chosen to govern in the name of their political faction. After what happened to my school, I quickly realized the Republican Party had become twisted by their pursuit of greed rather than the maintenance of order. While I'm sure such a corruption of values is not new to the Republican Party, or any party for that matter, it was a shock to my system and to the faith I had previously held in the political system. I now realize how easy it is to be swayed by false promises from those who have perfected manipulation of the public into an art form. This is not an attack solely on Republican leadership, however, as I believe the entire political system is broken and needs change, and I see that change when I look around at my classmates.

During the town hall held at the BB&T Center a week after

the shooting, which Representative Ted Deutch and Senators Bill Nelson and Marco Rubio attended, it became clear to me that the future generation truly is the generation with the capacity to make real change through real discussion. The development of society is founded on the principle of compromise and finding the middle ground; however, such a concept was shown to be lost in older generations when they allowed passion to overrule logic and turned to jeers and screams instead of hearing out their representatives. The passion many of the adults showed comes from the right place, but it does not suit the attempts to make real change. Instead, it allows those who would disagree with them to write them off as a faceless crowd unknowledgeable about issues and unwilling to listen to a dissenting opinion.

On the other hand, the children they have raised seem to be quite the opposite. So many people have heaped praise on my classmates and me for how we have acted in the wake of the massacre, regardless of political affiliation or the goals being pursued. To see my friends take the world of politics by storm has been an unreal experience. Witnessing the names of my classmates tied to projects that are bringing about real change in the world is something that I can't help but smile about. We really do appear to be the generation that will make the necessary changes to repair the failings of society, and the world we create in the wake of the legacy we leave is a world I'm excited to live in.

Photo by Ryan Deitsch

FROM VICTIMS TO VILLAINS

by Rebecca Schneid

We never wanted this attention, this fame. That is the first thing
you need to know about all of us. Every single person in this
school who received opportunities after the murder of our seventeen classmates and faculty members would give everything back
for this never to have happened. Often, my friends and I find
ourselves reminiscing about fun memories mere weeks before the
tragedy. And though we realize that we had our own issues, in-
securities, and sadness back then, it wasn't anything compared to
this hollowness we feel. We are seeing significant changes as a result of our work, not just in the form of policy, but also within the

minds of our nation's constituents. But by the same token, each stride we have taken has taken a piece of us with it.

The only people who understand the pain and anguish that led us into action are our peers. But so many others refused to see us as anything other than nuisances, and did whatever they could to tear us down. Mere days after the shooting, we were being called opportunists, and were accused of "taking the deaths of our friends and twisting it." It seemed like one day we were victims to be pitied by all of America, and the next, we were enemies of half the country. Sometimes we were called communists. Other times we were labeled crisis actors. Then, with head-spinning speed, memes and tweets appeared, accusing us of trying to rip up the Constitution (literally and figuratively). Confusingly, we were also shown as morons with no knowledge of politics or the world around us. The criticism, most of which were more like hurled insults with the purpose of causing us pain, seemed never ending.

My first experiences with the villainization of my classmates didn't come as a personal attack against me, but rather were direct hits on my closest friends who were out in the spotlight. My friends, who I had been in school with for years and years, were accused of being actors playing a role for the far left, or whoever employed them to participate in this performance about a school shooting that didn't actually happen.

Oh, how I wish that was the truth. I wish more than anything that this shooting was a lie. That my friends and I were hired to speak about our trauma for a political purpose. That we were actors getting paid for the tears we shed every single day. But that isn't the truth. The truth is that we *did* go through a shooting. Many of us *did* hide and run for our lives. Our friends *were* murdered in front of many of us. The truth is that many of us left school on Valentine's Day covered in our classmates' blood. No, that was not CGI or special effects trickery for a movie. It was all real, it was bloody, and it was a massacre. I would give everything I have for it to have been made up.

Those were some of the initial assaults used to distract the public from the message we were sending out, but they would certainly not be the last. One friend would sometimes cry to me about how people would brutally criticize her looks when she went on television to advocate for a safer future, something she was already insecure about. Emma González was criticized for her sexuality and appearance. David Hogg's face was put onto a shooting target and actually shot at in a video posted on Twitter. Delaney Tarr was sent hate mail calling her vulgar, despicable names. I talk about these bluntly because not only am I sure most of those following this issue have seen these attacks, but also because they are simple facts of how we have been victimized again after the shooting.

I would see the posts on Twitter and think: *Do these people think this is an appropriate way to speak to another human, let alone a teenage survivor of gun violence?* I was appalled, but I honestly did not let myself dwell on it too much. I showed anger online and was obviously upset, but I realized it was the work of the trolls that I had come to know throughout my experience online.

But that attitude would soon change when a similarly relentless hate campaign was directed toward me. I made a few appearances on several news networks like MSNBC and CNN, including CNN's *Reliable Sources,* in the days following the March For Our Lives. In these interviews, I talked about how our *Eagle Eye* reporters covered the march and how the students hoped to move forward with our activism by focusing on motivating young people to register to vote. Simply from the words "Stoneman Douglas student" appearing in front of my name, I received an onslaught of hate online, calling me anything from a blubbering idiot to a controlling communist (only one of which is true, by the way).

From my words on camera came almost 10,000 comments about how I was not, in fact, a reliable source (despite the name of the show) and had no validity. At a time when I was already struggling with the trauma and resulting heartbreak of the shooting, it was the last thing I needed. I was dealing with depression and anxiety, and then thousands of people spewed hateful things about my intelligence, looks, and home just from a few one-minute clips of me speaking on TV. Some of the comments were downright vulgar, making me wonder what kind of adult thinks it's okay to say such things to a sixteen-year-old shooting survivor, or any sixteen-year-old girl for that matter.

I was so confused. How did we as a community and March For Our Lives as an organization become the enemy of so many people just by advocating for some change in the world? It became obvious to me then that people were not listening to what was being said, and instead were making assumptions based on confirmation biases and fears about their rights.

So this was where compartmentalization came in as a useful tool. In order for me to do my job at the *Eagle Eye* and make the impact I hoped to, I had to shut all of it out. My friends who had been dealing with these insults and gross distortions of their positions since the beginning taught me to place the negativity in a little box and lock it away. I knew it would only distract me from the goal of preventing this violence from happening to anyone else's community, and I recognized that this was *exactly* what the trolls online wanted. They made up these fake stories, these reasons to hate us, so that we could be ignored or dismissed. People wouldn't listen to our message if it was covered in so much BS to mask it, right?

Wrong. We have all used this gross falsification of our lives and our views as fuel, trying even more vigorously to get our message across so people see through the lies. This nonsense is used to drag the eyes of the public away from what actually matters: the future. We refuse to let them win, always taking these smear stories and turning them back to our true mission of making our country a safer place for everyone, and empowering our youth to use their voices and their rights. I have decided to focus on the immense amount of love we have received from around the world to energize me and push me to work even harder toward our goal. The hate would only get in my way, and we have too much to accomplish!

EXTRAORDINARY ACTS

Freshman Chris McKenna Comes into Contact with Gunman Minutes Before Shooting

by Zoe Gordon

During the February 14 tragedy at Marjory Stoneman Douglas High School, some students and teachers helped save lives in the midst of chaos. Freshman Chris McKenna, who came into contact with the shooter minutes before he fired into the school, is one of those students.

McKenna was situated in room 1216 on the first floor of the Freshman Building. He asked English teacher Dara Hass if he could go to the bathroom, and then realized the one on his floor was locked, so he headed toward the bathroom on the second floor of the building. As McKenna opened the stairwell door leading him to the second floor, he locked eyes with the shooter, who was loading up his AR-15.

"When I saw him, he told me, 'You better get out of here. Things are going to get messy,'" McKenna said. "I was shocked, and I had a gut feeling of what he was about to do. My first instinct was to run."

McKenna rushed out of the Freshman Building and notified Coach Aaron Feis, who was soon to be one of the seventeen victims of the tragedy. At the time, Feis was unlocking the senior parking lot gate, but after hearing McKenna's warning, he took him on his golf cart to the baseball fields.

"He told me to stay there while he was going to check it out," McKenna said. "He went into the building and came out a hero."

Though Feis was shot in the Freshman Building, McKenna does not feel guilty about asking him for help. He knew he had to get help from someone, and Feis was the first person he encountered. McKenna later heard that Feis shielded other students in the building from the bullets, sacrificing his life for theirs.

"People are telling me that I did the right thing, and I feel like I did, too," McKenna said. "I could have been the first one gone if I tried to question [the shooter]. He had an AR-15 rifle right in his hand."

Although McKenna does not recognize himself as a hero, he considers Feis a true hero because he put others' lives before his own.

MANAGING YOUR OWN BIAS
IN REPORTING

by Suzanna Barna

Being a journalist and an activist do not go hand in hand; instead, the two tasks challenge each other until their lines blur, as we see daily in mainstream media. The blurring of these lines and the recent phenomenon of labeling journalists "fake news" have created distrust of the media.

It's important to realize that bias is natural. Through political socialization ("the process by which people acquire their political attitudes, beliefs, opinions, and behaviors," according to *Oxford Bibliographies*), everyone has been trained to think a certain way in their political opinions due to age, environment, friends, and parents' views. Like the saying goes, the first step to overcoming a problem is to recognize that there is one. By identifying one's own biases, it becomes easier to minimize those effects in writing and reporting.

I am aware that I lean slightly liberal and libertarian. I am quite moderate on most issues in politics, and although my parents are fairly conservative and I respect their politics, I've always been a free thinker and do not simply accept their stances. Instead, I have gained knowledge about the world and formed my own opinions. Because of my curious nature and my parents' views, I've gained the ability to understand all sides of a political issue.

Through the past months, I've used this trait as a superpower. Not only has this helped with interviews by guiding the questions toward the overall issues of gun reform and school safety instead of asking partisan-framed questions, but it has also impacted my reporting since the shooting. In journalism, objectivity has been a necessity.

When VICE News interviewed me and some friends, they slanted their questions to try to evoke an emotional response from us about President Trump and his lack of action and leadership since the shooting. Instead, we redirected the conversation to the issues rather than focusing on specific people, allowing us to contribute to finding real solutions to the complicated issue of gun violence and school shootings that the country needs. Adding to the screaming and yelling that circulates among most partisan politicians will not accomplish meaningful change.

When it came to journalism at the *Eagle Eye,* we were especially vigilant about avoiding our own biases when working on the last two issues of the year. With the memorial issue, we had no concerns about any political criticism—the issue was entirely dedicated to remembering the seventeen beautiful lives lost on Valentine's Day, as the name "In Memoriam" indicates. But in our last issue, "Taking a Stand," complaints seemed inevitable from some more conservative individuals who were unhappy with the school newspaper being political. Yet with unbiased reporting we hoped to minimize those complaints.

To keep from imposing our own viewpoints in "Taking a Stand," we chose to focus on the major events that have occurred since the tragedy at our school and shine light on the initiatives that have come about as a result. We had two March For Our Lives spreads that covered the march and what happened in Washington, D.C., and Parkland, Florida. In addition, we featured several initiatives for activism and awareness, including Change the Ref, a nonprofit organization created by Joaquin Oliver's parents to empower youth and "help lead the way to change—a more peaceful future"; Meadow's Movement, an organization created in honor of Meadow Pollack to advocate for policy change and create a playground in Meadow's memory; and Stories Untold, an initiative to share a variety of experiences about events on February 14 and other shooting incidents, from people who haven't gotten as much attention from the media.

We aimed to avoid toxic voices who only wanted to echo the predominant partisan politics. By establishing this standard, we sought to include members of the community who have risen above their differences in a rallying cry for change.

The *Eagle Eye* also tried to keep the last issue focused on gun reform and school safety, instead of discussing individuals. As we worked on this issue, I saw that we had more articles about gun violence, statistics, and solutions than we did about school safety measures and their effectiveness. I personally wished our coverage was a bit more balanced and discussed school safety more.

One of the subtle but significant ways to minimize bias in reporting is through word choice and framing. In this aspect, the *Eagle Eye* works tirelessly to write about facts more than feelings in the articles we publish. Instead of using biased slang terms or slanting the writing to represent one side of the argument over another, the *Eagle Eye* uses three rounds of editing for each article to catch any charged language before it is considered ready for publishing.

With our thoroughness and awareness, the *Eagle Eye* has strived throughout this chaotic period to maintain our high standards for objectivity, and I am proud to be a staffer on our school's news publication.

Photo by Suzanna Barna

SPEAKING OUT FOR THOSE WHO CAN'T

by Delaney Tarr

From the moment we were led from our school by SWAT teams, we immediately went from shaken victims to media celebrities. There was never really any time to grieve. As journalism students, we had an idea of how the media would cover the story that is our lives. There would be a horde of cameras during those first few days, clamoring for the most emotional story. And over time, they would fade away. Sure, it wasn't what we wanted, but it was the reality we were faced with, as even hours after the tragedy, news outlets were competing for interviews. Most of us were angry, we were grieving, and we were heartbroken. It was hard to even get out of bed, much less confront the journalists who would never know what the experience was like.

Yet that was what propelled us into action. Having all these people, with rapt attention, waiting to see what we had to say, waiting to understand how we felt, presented us with a strange situation. Yes, we were grieving, and yes, we just wanted to be with each other, but there were all these people camped outside our school, our town, our homes, just waiting for us to talk. Ready for us to say something, anything.

Not everyone was ready to talk, though. Those in the freshman building, those more directly affected, simply were not ready to face the mountain of press that had built up around our school. And that's understandable. It was intimidating, the endless flood of direct messages and phone calls we were receiving. After one interview, it seemed all of the media would have your contact information, and they never stopped calling. For many, it was too much, and they had to take a step back.

That was where a level of instinct kicked in among some of us. Knowing myself, and knowing that I had experience being on camera for the TV production newscast, for both interviewing and being interviewed through newspaper and TV, I felt an obligation to speak out. If I knew how to stay composed on camera, didn't I have a responsibility to use my voice? So many of our peers weren't ready to use their voices, but I was. Many of the students speaking up were journalists, drama performers, debaters, and student government representatives.

Well, as ready as we could be. We were grieving, too. In many ways, speaking out was our form of grieving. It let us process our emotions, get our stories out there. It helped us feel like at least one person was listening to our pain, even if it was just the journalist. But we also understood the way the news media worked.

Every journalism student realized that the cameras were waiting for a story, and somebody had to give it to them. So we gave them what they wanted. I scheduled an interview with UK Channel 4 for the day of the vigil and spoke to them between fits of sobbing. That first interview was so raw, so real, but it was only the first in a series of press interactions that would soon dominate our lives.

Even through all the tears and pain of those first few interviews, I recognized I was in a unique place. The only time I felt composed in any way was during those interviews, a sentiment many of my journalist peers shared. We were comforting ourselves by doing something that was so familiar; it almost felt like home.

The day after the shooting, and every day after that, we threw ourselves into work. We made ourselves known to the media; we became the representatives of a much larger population. It was by no means intentional, but somebody needed to fill the role. Why not the people who could stomach it?

While we worked, others took the time to focus on healing. It was such an important thing to do, so vital to health, but we couldn't necessarily do it. At least, not in the way we should have. Instead, we'd send out a fiery tweet or speak to our legislators as our therapeutic acts.

Of course, we also recognized that the attention was temporary. As time passed, others wanted their voices to be heard, so we stepped back to let them speak out. We tried to propel their platforms by connecting them to the ones we had built. We wanted

to give a voice to people who were so much closer to the tragedy, like Sam Fuentes, who had been shot and was now healing.
These were the voices we amplified because they were the ones
that *needed* to be heard.

They're the ones we continue to promote every day, as we
learn more and more about how many others have been affected
by gun violence. We learn of people who have been silenced by
the pull of a trigger, by murder. We learn to use our voices to
channel theirs, to speak for those who will never be able to speak
again. For our own peers, for our seventeen Eagles, who no longer have a voice of their own. We are their vessel, making sure the
world remembers them and is forced to acknowledge all that was
lost in those quick and terrible moments of violence.

NOT JUST A WALK TO THE PARK

Covering Civil Disobedience

by Christy Ma

The national walkout that swept schools—even schools hundreds of miles away from Marjory Stoneman Douglas—was inspiring and something I was honored to report on. It was March 14, the one-month anniversary of the shooting that changed our lives forever, and MSD planned a schoolwide walkout to the football field in response to the violence and the inaction of legislators. I was assigned to report on the walkout that morning, which had nearly the entire student population of 3,300 on the field on that sunny, fateful day.

Being on the shorter end physically, I was lucky to have fellow newspaper staffers taking pictures for my story, especially of the crowds. Participating in the walkout, but also observing the events that occurred during the walkout, was particularly difficult. I would find myself feeling the inevitable raw emotions along with my classmates, but the development of the story was in the back of my mind, so I had to balance this task with my emotions. I had to be there for my friends, while also remembering the sequence of events and the details of the day.

There were rumors of MSD students taking the walkout beyond the barriers of the school grounds, something Principal Thompson did not endorse but which felt very right for my peers. Although I was assigned to just report on the walkout at school, I followed my instincts to continue with the march and exit campus to Pine Trails Park, almost two miles away, because I knew the story of MSD students wanting to take it farther— wanting to demonstrate that keeping the hurt and anguish inside those fences was impossible—was a story the *Eagle Eye* could tell the best.

To be frank, I was nervous. I'm what you'd call a Goody Two-shoes, and skipping class is something I would never think to do, especially when taking challenging AP courses and being fearful of missing essential information and class time. However, the weight of the story outmatched my need to be in class, and I knew that I was witnessing the start of a history of change for MSD, and for students across the nation who were taking a stance, screaming that enough is enough. Gun violence in America has become the norm, and the nation's youth are tired of it. I wanted to do my part and give my peers the platform for their voices to be amplified, and to show the world how resilient the next generation is.

My decision to leave campus to report the events outside the school was, in a way, my point of no return. As soon as I stepped out of those red gates, I knew I could only go all in with my reporting, and I witnessed outside media outlets taking this opportunity to tell our stories as well.

People underestimate the effort it takes to speed-walk and talk, but it was a feat journalists at the walkout had to overcome. I had to approach students from all grades, including our neighboring middle school students who decided to join us to support our effort. Lacking an actual notepad, pen, and even a camera due to my spontaneous decision to follow the crowd off-campus, I had to improvise by texting my newspaper classmates to see if a photographer was walking off-campus, too, and immediately typed questions on my phone's notepad to ask walkout participants what the event meant to them. It was chaotic but worthwhile, because the raw emotions were captured as I acquired valuable quotes and information from strangers and speakers at the park.

As soon as I returned to the newspaper classroom, it was crunch time. The story needed to be published before school ended, because online stories about events of this magnitude had to be posted in a timely manner. So I spent the rest of my seventh period and lunchtime writing the story. Going through the audio recordings and notes on my phone was an obstacle in itself, but was possible with enough focus and determination. My files and notes were disorganized due to the spontaneity of the event, so I had to decipher bulleted notes and audio files without titles.

Sitting in the newspaper room and witnessing the hashtag trend on Twitter for #NationalSchoolWalkout was also inspiring to see, and to know that I published a story on it was rewarding.

The school was starting a nationwide movement, and we even received pictures from other Broward County schools and out-of-state schools that were standing by MSD and participating in their own walkouts. I decided to feature a photo from Deerfield Beach High School, a nearby school, that was an aerial view of students spelling #MSDStrong. Seeing the support on that day was uplifting, and this generation needs to keep the spark going.

Reporting on something that held so much emotional value and weight for me was difficult, and would have been difficult for any journalist, but I'm proud that my friends have been able to pull through together in order to give the world an example of a school that won't back down in the midst of tragedy, and will keep pushing forward to a future of hope.

EXTRAORDINARY ACTS

Senior Kelly Plaur Protects Her Teacher from Gunfire

by Nyan Clarke

On February 14, 2018, in the face of unimaginable danger, many students and teachers emerged as heroes to their community. While bullets flew into her classroom, senior Kelly Plaur acted on her instincts to help her peers. She had no idea these instincts would cause her peers to deem her a hero.

Plaur was sitting in Ivy Schamis's Holocaust history class in room 1214 when she heard three loud bangs coming from outside the classroom. Recognizing them as gunshots, Plaur and her classmates immediately ran for cover.

The class split into separate hiding groups, with Plaur first taking cover against a wall near her teacher's desk with a group of her classmates and Schamis. Looking around the room, Plaur realized her teacher was not completely covered by the desk.

"There was nowhere to hide in the classroom, which really sucks, and Mrs. Schamis didn't really have anywhere to go," Plaur said. "I remember looking around, seeing her and thinking about my mom."

As she sat against the wall, Plaur noticed her teacher texting someone that she loved them, but the text would not go through. Feeling the need to protect her teacher, Plaur pulled Schamis in between her legs, giving her more coverage in case the shooter entered the classroom.

"I wanted to protect her because I knew she had kids of her own and a husband. I was thinking, 'What if this was my mom?' So I knew I just had to protect her because she would do the same for me if I couldn't fit somewhere," Plaur said.

Plaur and Schamis huddled together, holding each other's hand, still unsure if what they heard in the hall was firecrackers or actual gunshots. Plaur called the police as soon as the shooting started, making her the first student to do so. She told the 911 operator what was happening, where she was, and that kids were injured.

"I told them I'm CPR-certified, but they were telling me I can't move, I can't help them, because [the 911 operator] said if the police [saw] me from outside through the window, it could've been an issue," Plaur said. "They'll think I could be the suspect."

Minutes passed, and the police finally arrived at Plaur's class and escorted the injured students out of the classroom. Plaur and Schamis both got out unharmed.

While Schamis is grateful for her student's actions, Plaur herself holds remorse toward her inability to help those who were injured in her class.

"It bothers me that I couldn't help [the injured]," Plaur said.

Though Plaur's empathy and quick thinking kept her and Schamis out of harm's way, she believes being called a "hero" is an overstatement. "I don't consider myself a hero because I don't need a title to know what I did [was right]."

TWEETING FOR CHANGE
An Interview with Carlitos Rodriguez

by Daniella Infantino

Carlitos Rodriguez is a seventeen-year-old completing his junior year at Marjory Stoneman Douglas High School. He was born in Venezuela and moved here with his parents and three siblings when he was eight years old. Carlitos is involved in the community and the school as the historian of Spanish Club. At MSD, Carlitos found a love for television production and could always be spotted with a camera producing YouTube vlogs about his life. To Carlitos and his family, Parkland seemed like the most secure place to move to, until the Stoneman Douglas mass shooting on

Valentine's Day made the city infamous. Carlitos wanted to use his video background to help heal the community by giving a voice to those whose stories have been untold. Carlitos's stories can be found through Twitter at @StoriesUntoldUS.

Daniella: Where were you on this day?
Carlitos: On February 14, I was in the office thanks to Mr. Porter, one of the administrators. Originally, I was in the Spanish room with Mr. Acosta, but when we were going downstairs, my class went ahead and got out of the school before me.

Daniella: Did you hear anything in the office?
Carlitos: We heard a couple shots and then a scream.

Daniella: Did you have any idea what was happening?
Carlitos: As soon as I walked downstairs, I saw Ms. Paula (guidance counselor) and she was crying, so I knew something was really wrong. Then I saw Mr. Porter when he brought us in the office, and he started locking every door, so I had a feeling that there was a shooter on campus.

Daniella: Do you have any friends that were impacted?
Carlitos: Yeah, Anthony Borges, Daniela Menescal, Joaquin Oliver, Coach Feis, Coach Hixon.

Daniella: What have you been doing since this tragedy occurred at Marjory Stoneman Douglas?
Carlitos: I have been working on @StoriesUntoldUS, which is a Twitter page that amplifies the voices of people who were there

but feel silenced and people who want to be heard. Right now, our main focus is people who have been affected by gun violence because we want to show our support for the March For Our Lives movement and impact the midterm elections this November.

Daniella: What is the overall goal of Stories Untold?

Carlitos: We are sharing the survivors' stories, and we are also doing call-to-actions, specifically for this November to get out and vote. In these call-to-actions, people bring messages about gun violence and they share a little bit about how they have been affected by it and why it needs to stop.

Daniella: One of the students you focused a lot on is Anthony Borges. How did that come about, and how has that impacted your storytelling?

Carlitos: My friend Anthony was shot and he is a really good friend of mine. We spent Christmas together and we spent New Year's together. When I heard the news, I was in a state of confusion. I didn't understand, and I didn't quite process that Anthony was shot. It wasn't until the day that I saw him in the hospital that I understood his condition. When I saw him, he was so skinny, you could see the veins on his chest, you could just see the vulnerability that us humans have, and it made me realize that it could happen to anyone. Anthony, a Venezuelan like me, moved here two years ago looking for safety, and then he encountered this. It made me realize that voices like his need to be heard because a lot of the media right now is focused on a set amount of people, a little group, but in reality, there are thousands of suppressed and silenced voices around the country that deserve to be heard.

Daniella: What are your other motivations for starting this page?

Carlitos: Before all this happened, I had a YouTube channel. I posted my first video on April 8, 2014. It always used to be for fun. I started out with my iPad, and I would bring it outside and skateboard with it. Around two years ago I bought a camera and decided to vlog about my life. I made a video the last day of school my freshman year that got a bit of attention, so I decided to start bringing my camera consistently and vlog my high school experience. I developed a passion for television production, and I channeled it to the Twitter page that I have now.

Daniella: How have you searched out the people you have interviewed?

Carlitos: A lot of the people we interview actually reach out to us because they want their stories to be heard. They email us and they ask us if they could be interviewed, if we could go to where they're at, or if they could come here. Sandy Hook Promise, a local organization, reached out to us the first day that we launched, so hopefully soon we will be going to Connecticut. We also have had the opportunity to interview Columbine survivors through the Jefferson County Students for a [sic] Change, and we went to Colorado.

Daniella: What was memorable about the Columbine interviews?

Carlitos: We spoke to them and they gave us advice about our emotions and how to deal with this situation since they have had nineteen years to rebuild their community while we have only had three months. Instead of sharing their experiences and sharing call-to-actions, they wanted to tell us about how they dealt with their experience afterward. Their situation was a bit different. [Douglas student] Darian Williams and I came up with questions about how they were feeling because we know a lot of them continue to be affected by the shooting nineteen years later. A lot of the questions were along the lines of "How can we rise up from this?" or "How can we heal?"

Daniella: What do you do with these stories?
Carlitos: We edit them and upload them onto our Twitter page, @StoriesUntoldUS.

Daniella: What kinds of questions do you ask your interviewees?
Carlitos: It depends. When it has to do with experiences, we let them talk and say what they want. We let them just express themselves and let it out. We don't like to interrupt them when it comes to their experience because that's something very delicate. If they want us out of the room, we go out. It depends on where we are and the situation. With call-to-actions, we give them a little structure of what they could say. If they have something written out, they can express themselves how they want. We ultimately try to end them with the same purpose so they all have the same messages getting across.

Daniella: In hearing these stories, what has surprised you?
Carlitos: Every single story gives me goose bumps, especially the ones from Stoneman Douglas because it's my home. Hearing my friends' stories keeps me wondering and keeps me thinking about what could have happened or "What could I have done?" and just "Why did this have to happen?"

Daniella: Do you think these stories help people cope with their personal experience with gun violence?

Carlitos: Yes, most definitely. People hear these stories and, if they live through it, they associate with it and feel encouraged to speak out. This Twitter page isn't just here to cause a change in November; it is here to help communities. @StoriesUntoldUS is a means for people to share stories and include everyone. We don't want to push anybody to the side or belittle their experience because even if they weren't in the building or if they weren't shot, they might still be affected.

Daniella: How do you feel about your progress?

Carlitos: I think Stories Untold has had a lot of success. It is different for me because I used to post happy things, but now this is more serious. Stories Untold has a message and a goal. We don't just want to reach 10,000 people; we want to reach hundreds of thousands of people.

Daniella: Do you ever lose hope? And what would you say to those who are losing hope as well?

Carlitos: I most definitely lose hope. The future is unpredictable, and I don't know what is going to happen next. I'm not expecting to know what comes next, but I pray upon it because even though hope isn't clear at the moment, it isn't something we should lose. It is something we should hold on to because it helps us emotionally and it gives us something to look forward to.

HOLDING POLITICIANS TO ACCOUNT

by Ryan Deitsch

After the horrific murder of seventeen innocent people at Marjory
Stoneman Douglas High School in Parkland, Florida, several students, including myself, formed a group and multiple voices came
together to have one voice and one message. This group preached
the words "Never Again" in an effort to save any other community from encountering the tragedy that occurs when hordes of
innocent people face a death that nobody can justify. We need immediate change in our society, be it through legislation, better law
enforcement, or more safety in our schools. Change must come,

and it must come yesterday. We were failed by most of the people who were supposed to protect us, and we cannot allow chinks in our armor to remain unfixed after they've been identified.

Through the efforts of students like Cameron Kasky and Jaclyn Corin, we were able to reach our government in their legislatures, hoping to change their particular stances so other communities do not become crippled like ours. We arrived by the busload at our state capital, only to be disappointed as our legislature refused to meet with us and decided to focus on the more pressing matters of God and pornography, as they worked to pass legislation on those issues instead of issues of gun violence.

We raced back from Tallahassee to attend a town hall meeting on February 22. In attendance were Democratic Representative Ted Deutch, Senators Marco Rubio and Bill Nelson, Broward County Sheriff Scott Israel, and NRA national spokesperson Dana Loesch. This was the first time I had ever met an actual politician. I had to keep my composure as these very people are the ones who failed to take action after the many mass shootings in the United States, including the one at Sandy Hook Elementary. It was due to political inaction that no tools were in place to protect us in the event that a school shooting happened again.

We wanted to know why. Why didn't one adult or politician find a way to overcome their differences so they could do something that would stop this plague on our nation? It turns out that many politicians, and even more lobbyists, take money from the NRA. Here are some sobering facts: "If you add together all of the NRA's contributions to candidates, political parties, and political action committees between 1998 and 2016, it comes to more than

$13 million," according to calculations from the Center for Responsive Politics. Also, if you add up all their political and lobbying contributions, the NRA has spent $203.2 million on political activities since 1998.

We researched the candidates and discovered that Marco Rubio had taken $600,000 from the NRA. I couldn't wait to ask him my question at our town hall: Why do we as children or young adults have to march on Washington, D.C., to save our lives?

That is where I learned what political dancing was. I am sure you have seen on multiple news shows when a politician is asked a question and he or she doesn't answer but hijacks the interview to get out their own agenda to the public. The original question goes unanswered. This happened on the stage right in front of me, and I was powerless to stop it. I was so stunned, I don't remember what he actually said. I just know that it had nothing to do with what I asked.

Senator Rubio was also asked by another student if he would stop taking money from the NRA in the future, and he refused to give a clear answer no matter how hard he was pressed. This happened over and over again throughout the event.

On February 28, 2018, with the assistance of Representative Ted Deutch and his staff, we were given the chance to take ten students to Washington to meet with over 200 congresspeople, including representatives and senators. There were two people who really stood out to me at those meetings.

The first lawmaker I met, Congressman Sean Patrick Maloney of New York, was one of the most memorable. He taught us that a nation is only as strong as its weakest laws, and if the law is weak, it will be subject to loopholes making it even weaker.

There were so many great meetings, but the other lawmaker that made a big impression on me was Congressman John Lewis. Congressman Lewis was one of the organizers of the Selma to Montgomery March in Alabama in March 1965. He is seventy-eight years old. After many years his voice still resonates with his passion for equality. The most memorable thing he said at our meeting was " 'Good trouble' is the idea that you must stand up for what is right, and if you get arrested it doesn't make you a criminal." Congressman Lewis has been arrested. He was also beaten for seeking equality. It didn't make him a bad person; it made him a congressman—eventually.

Throughout this whole activist process, I have come to feel that politicians hold little regard for their constituents. They make empty promises, and this goes all the way up the chain to President Donald Trump. In front of our nation and in front of grieving parents, the president promised a ban on bump stocks, which is a part that can be added to an assault rifle, like the one used in the mass shooting in Las Vegas, to make it mimic a fully automatic weapon. But he has done nothing to bring about that change so far. How disappointing.

Our meeting with Senator Rubio was another letdown. He was not prepared and seemed completely flustered. He couldn't recall his position on several issues and snapped angrily at his staffers, asking them for answers he should have known about his position on issues. By the end of our town hall meeting, we thought he had taken steps toward our side of the issue. But now it seemed like when he was off that stage and out of the public eye, that change of heart never happened.

We must hold our lawmakers to account and insist that they do the work that we've elected them to do. And we must make sure that young people vote, so our voices are heard and we help elect leaders who support the issues that are important to us.

SHINING A LIGHT ON GUN VIOLENCE
Diverse Perspectives

by Richard Doan

Marjory Stoneman Douglas High is a suburban school of 3,300 students located in the affluent, mostly white community of Parkland, Florida. However, the demographics of the surrounding community don't fully represent the diversity within the classrooms of MSD. Much like the United States as a whole, Marjory Stoneman Douglas High is a melting pot of countless nations, languages, and traditions. Although whites do make up a majority at 59 percent of students, black, Hispanic, Asian, and American Indian populations comprise the remaining 41 percent.

Each ethnic background is highlighted and celebrated annually at the Multicultural World Showcase. This popular school event celebrates MSD's diverse and talented students in dancing, singing, acting, and spoken-word poetry from different cultures across the globe. The performances not only evoke national pride and charm the audience, but also bring together a team of students with an appreciation for the world and its cultures. Our school's union of different perspectives and identities enhances the intellectual, emotional, moral, and spiritual life of our student body. Though we vary in appearance and culture, we are bound together by our undeniable pride to be Eagles.

In a diverse school of 3,300, the tragic loss of seventeen lives has a way of making a large student body feel drastically smaller and emptier. From the horrors of darkness and evil, our community is left with tears and broken hearts. But this is not our story. Our tale will not be defined by the cruel acts of the wicked, but rather in the impact of our response.

While the community grieves and prays, some turn toward political activism for solace. We speak out against the devastation that gun violence inflicts. We ask, "How many more?" until our representatives take action. Together, we've created the popular #NeverAgain movement and March For Our Lives, which rapidly gained traction nationwide.

Understandably, however, not all MSD students believe in the platforms of these publicly acclaimed (and criticized) movements. In a school of 3,300 students, people can expect that the controversial issue of gun violence and reform can elicit a range of opinions and viewpoints. It is safe to say that although many students may fully support the March For Our Lives platform, there are individuals with divergent beliefs.

In the midst of the liberal-leaning March For Our Lives platform, there is another important stance at MSD to be acknowledged: the conservative voice. These individuals do not argue for high-capacity magazine and assault weapon bans, but rather for alternative solutions to end school shootings. MSD junior Patrick Petty, for instance, is passionate about finding solutions for school safety while defending the Second Amendment. Although we all strive for safer school environments, Petty admits that he does not always agree with his classmates who started the March For Our Lives movement.

"I know that their fear is that they'll get bashed for their views, and I think that's the fear on the pro–Second Amendment side, on the more conservative side," Petty said in an interview with WLRN.

Petty certainly is not alone in his political stance. Across the spectrum, some are understandably nervous about expressing their opinions on guns. Even when we agree that change is necessary, we often have differing opinions on what that change should be.

MSD junior Kyle Kashuv, for instance, catapulted onto the national stage as a conservative counterweight to the Parkland students who advocate for more stringent gun-control laws. Kashuv's focus, rather, is centered on increasing school security and expanding background checks (especially for mental health). Kashuv explained in a Fox News interview that he firmly believes that "guns aren't the issue," but that "everything surrounding acquiring a weapon" is the real problem at hand.

"The initial movement, in its purest form, was amazing. It got corrupted because now it's represented as anti-gun and anti-NRA. 'Boycott this, boycott that.' It's detracting from the actual discussions," Kashuv said.

The media has placed a particular emphasis on the left vs. right nature of the gun-control debate. The ubiquity of this discussion on air and in print leaves many others feeling left out of the conversation, even though their voices are just as important.

Twelve percent of MSD's student body is black, but one wouldn't be able to tell from the school's media coverage. At a press conference on March 28, some African American students in Parkland, including junior Kai Koerber, said they have been underrepresented by both the media and some of their peers leading the conversation for gun reform. March For Our Lives organizers have called out the media for their underrepresentation and have brought minority students from MSD onto their summer Road to Change tour throughout Florida.

Another major concern for these African American students is that some of the solutions designed to keep them safer actually make them feel even more afraid than before. Much like the rest of us students, Koerber came back to school after the shooting to see the empty desks of our fallen Eagles transformed into memorials. Already distressed and startled, he also returned to a campus overrun with law enforcement. To Koerber, the elevated police presence at school doesn't mean that there are more people to protect him; it means that there are more chances for him to be a victim of police brutality. He fears that the police will racially profile him and other students of color and regard them as potential criminals.

It is extremely important to recognize all voices and perspectives along the political spectrum. Yet many stories are left unheard. The African American students at MSD have shared and continue to share their stories in light of their underrepresentation in the media.

The underrepresentation of diverse voices is paralleled on the national scale in regard to urban gun violence. There are schools and communities that have been suffering from shootings for much longer and much more often than the people of South Florida have, yet their voices often go unnoticed. The students from southern Los Angeles and the South Side of Chicago, for instance, fear for their lives daily because of the gun violence that plagues their communities. Their struggles do not usually make the national news, but it represents a more common form of gun violence in America.

These urban communities are places where gun violence is rather typical. It is, in a way, a fact of life. Homicide after homicide fails to grab the attention that a seemingly random mass shooting at a school, church, or theater draws. The national conversation tends to brush over these areas where gun violence runs rampant.

In Boston, more than half of all gun violence cases are concentrated within less than 3 percent of the streets and intersections of the area. According to a study in the *Journal of Quantitative Criminology,* these incidents "seem to be the primary drivers of overall gun violence trends in Boston." The horrors of gun violence are most prevalent in disadvantaged urban neighborhoods, where homicide rates reach more than ten times the national average, according to a PICO National Network report.

"This is happening over and over again," Zion Kelly, a senior at Thurgood Marshall Academy in Washington, D.C., said in his speech at the March For Our Lives. "Dozens of students have been shot and killed—more than in Florida—and we're not getting the same attention." Kelly's twin brother, Zaire, was shot and killed in September 2017.

For urban communities, it is difficult to hear the tone of the gun violence conversation resonating on a different wavelength, especially when it is directed largely to the white middle class. For them, their misery of gun violence is different. Their tears and bloodshed are in a steady, relentless rhythm rather than disparate eruptions of mass murder.

The bulk of the nation's gun violence is caused by a very small group of people. America's high rate of gun murders is not due to events like Parkland or Sandy Hook, but is rather driven by the relentless deaths of blacks in urban communities. The majority of these shootings do not affect most affluent white Americans because so many of them take place in impoverished, minority, urban areas. Even though only about 13 percent of the general population is black, more than half of the murder victims in 2016 were black, with 73 percent of them murdered by guns, according to FBI homicide data.

Nonetheless, legislatures have long regarded this crisis as a societal norm. Michael McBride, a pastor who has been a strong advocate for programs that reduce urban violence, credits this oversight to the fact that it is blacks and not whites who are the primary victims, according to a lengthy feature on McBride in *ProPublica*. Data from the Centers for Disease Control and Prevention supports this striking disparity, as "black Americans are, on average, eight times more likely to be killed by firearms than those who are white." According to a public health study at Boston University, "the black homicide rate for urban areas in Missouri was higher than the total death rate from any cause in New York State [in 2015]."

Mass shootings, on the other hand, feel different. People

believe that they can take place anywhere, so they feel like a more plausible threat. Aside from local news, the everyday deaths in urban communities rarely receive much media coverage, and most of the public rarely seems to take notice.

There is a distinction between the experiences of an urban community member and one from a suburban area. Unlike mass shootings, urban gun violence has long been accepted as the usual, largely due to its ubiquity.

"Chicago has been plagued with gun violence since long before the Parkland shooting," Young Urban Progressives member Juan Reyes said in his speech at the Chicago March For Our Lives. "Suddenly, people are talking about students not feeling safe in schools. But in reality, students in our city's South and West Side have never felt safe."

The students in the urban communities of D.C. share similar sentiments of their interminable fear of gun violence. Whether they are in their front yard or on the playground, they fear that they will be next to fall victim to an assailant's bullet.

"In D.C., they're always bringing up housing and real estate [in the news]. But they never bring up gun violence," Thurgood Marshall Academy senior Ramsey Williams said in an interview in the *Washington Post*. "And now that people are talking about what happened in Florida, we're thinking, 'We feel like that all the time.'"

Schools across the country hosted student-organized walkouts in support of the grieving Parkland community. The #NeverAgain efforts culminated in the March For Our Lives, which brought together millions of activists in Washington, D.C., New York, and all around the country. The march unified the efforts of the nation to raise awareness of this uniquely American issue.

Although the struggles of urban communities have been largely overlooked, the March For Our Lives sought to elevate these voices to the international stage. At the march, the focus of concern extended beyond the mass shootings at suburban schools like Marjory Stoneman Douglas High School to include the pervasive gun violence in urban areas. The inclusiveness of the event unified the plight of all those afflicted by gun violence into one central movement for change. For the powerless and the overlooked, for the neglected and ignored, it was their chance to finally be heard. Whether real action is made in response to their activism remains uncertain.

I believe that this nation needs not a heated political argument, but a respectful discussion about guns and mental health. Each side must be willing to listen to the opinions of the other side.

Through bipartisanship and working across the political aisle, I believe it can happen. I believe in compromise. Practically everyone recognizes that there is a need for change. Though people have their own views on how to enact such change, such divergence can foster intelligent discussion and the exploration of all possible options. But we must let all viewpoints be heard and acknowledged.

I believe most people feel we need to pass some commonsense gun laws. I believe we can agree that we must keep guns out of the hands of those who show signs of malicious intent. I believe we can agree on widening the information stored in background check databases and increasing restrictions on the acquisition of firearms for the mentally ill. From there, we'll work to ensure the safety of our nation's children without sacrificing the liberties the foundation of America grants us.

Change can be daunting, and not all changes work. But doing nothing isn't going to solve anything. Let us set aside our political differences to work together. Let us initiate change for the common cause of the preservation of life. Let us use our hindsight as foresight and shape a better future.

It didn't happen after Columbine in 1999, but it will happen now, and the students of Marjory Stoneman Douglas will be the ones behind it. It is all to save a life—maybe even seventeen, and hopefully more.

EXTRAORDINARY ACTS

Psychology Teacher Ronit Reoven Provides First Aid to Injured Students

by Einav Cohen

In fourth period on February 14, AP Psychology teacher Ronit Reoven was giving a lesson on psychologist Sigmund Freud and the psychosexual stages of development. Reoven looked at the clock to see how much time she had left to teach; it was a few minutes past 2:15, almost dismissal time.

Two minutes later, deafening booms came from the hallway outside. Startled, the students sprang out of their desks and ran away from the door toward the windows on the other side of the classroom.

"They were trying to get to the side of the glass window.

I stopped them and made them go to the right side. 'Go behind my desk, go behind my desk,'" Reoven told her students.

As the third classroom that was targeted, thankfully, the students had enough time to listen to Reoven's directions and hide along the wall that shared the door to the hallway.

"Mind you, I have thirty-one students; that's a lot to get to fit along the wall where the classroom door is. They squeezed in, huddled, laid on top of each other, whatever they could on that wall," Reoven said.

Reoven and her students could not see the gunman at any point as he shot into the room through the window on the door. She waited until there was nothing but silence in the hallway so she could assess what had happened to her students. Four students on the outskirts of the wall had been hit; three had been wounded, but the fourth tragically passed away inside the classroom. As she assessed her students' condition, she realized one had an arm wound that needed immediate treatment. Using a baby blanket her students passed to her from the top of her class coffeemaker, Reoven wrapped the student's wound, creating a makeshift tourniquet.

For the other two injured students, she could see that one was stable, and the other had multiple wounds. Reoven decided that not moving the students would be the best option.

After taking care of her students, Reoven listened through the closet to hear the activity happening in the hall. She wanted to get the authorities' attention, so she stood by the broken window until she could hear them coming.

In the midst of everything, one student, senior Harrison Albert, had been able to reach 911 and had been talking with them since the beginning of the attack. Albert told the police everything that was going on, and eventually the dispatcher let him know that authorities were on the way.

As much as Reoven helped her students, she says her students helped her, too, staying at her side, listening to her, and staying calm and quiet.

"As weird as it might sound, I was looking for strength from the kids as much as they were looking to me," Reoven said. "I don't know how I did what I did, to be honest. . . . I did what I could, and I did what I needed to do."

Reoven emphasized how one student, junior Logan Mitchell, was able to calm her down throughout the whole experience.

"[Logan] was my voice of reason. He would sit next to me, look at me in the eye. He would tell me, 'It's okay, it's going to be okay,' repeatedly. . . . He was with me," Reoven said.

Once the SWAT team had arrived and entered the Freshman Building, Reoven stuck her head out of the broken glass window on the classroom door to call for them urgently, saying she had injured students. The SWAT officers quickly picked up the injured and ran outside to the ambulances with them one by one. Then they allowed Reoven and her other students to get to safety across the street. All three of the injured students survived.

Reoven's extraordinary act of calling her students to turn around and hide against the wall by the classroom door saved many lives. MSD and the Parkland community appreciate and recognize Reoven and her students' courage and heroism during the tragedy of Valentine's Day.

COPING WITH TRAUMA WHILE KEEPING EMOTIONS IN CHECK

by Rebecca Schneid

From the moment this shooting occurred, I knew that the newspaper would be immensely important in my healing process. I did not yet understand the extent of it, but I was immediately tied to it, as the newspaper room was where I was during the shooting. The class that was once my home became the site of the most traumatic experience of my life. The closet where I used to go to eat lunch or watch videos with my friends was now the closet where I texted my mom goodbye, thinking I was going to die; it was where I hugged my friends goodbye; it was where my best friend used my shirt to muffle her cries; it was where I lost all of my innocence.

Obviously, that event was extremely confusing and traumatizing. But I still spend every day in the classroom, working on the newspaper that I love. And every day I remember a new small thing from February 14. Like last week I remembered how I was watching Vine compilations with my friends Delaney and Emma minutes before the shooting. Or I will remember running out of the room with my hands up, my Valentine's Day flowers in one hand and my computer in the other. In the chaos, most times I forget why I took the flowers with me in the first place, but then I remember that I wanted something to remind me of light and love in a time of such darkness.

Essentially, that day will always be tied with Newspaper. Furthermore, my experiences after the shooting will always be tied with Newspaper, since that is where I found my outlet. Immediately after the shooting, I drove home with my mom, sobbing uncontrollably, then sat in front of the television for about twelve hours straight, doing nothing but texting my friends to see who had died and who had survived, as I watched the events unfold on the news. There, I saw my Newspaper teacher, Mrs. Falkowski, the woman who hid me and eighteen other students in her closet, keeping us calm and declining calls from her own mother in order to keep it together for us.

Mrs. Falkowski was the most selfless woman I have ever met, and there she was on television, continuing to sacrifice for her students in order to plead for change. That same night, I texted her one thing: "Thank you for all that you did for me. I promise you, we will use our newspaper to fight for the people we lost. We will use it to change the world."

The next few days were a blur—vigils and interviews and rallies, and talk of the kind of change I never even could have dreamt of. But soon I came back to reality with our first editorial meeting one week and one day after the shooting at MSD—we were the storytellers in this. This was our story to report, and it was our job to tell it. Not only were we going to tell the story of Marjory Stoneman Douglas High School and the activism born out of it, but we were going to tell the stories of our fallen seventeen fellow Eagles.

So, in the midst of dealing with funerals, talks with politicians, interviews with *Time* and the *New York Times,* a breakup, and PTSD symptoms, I was suddenly a journalist reporting on the tragedy at my school, involving my friends and the death of my peers. I had a weight on my shoulder that I don't think I have ever felt in my life.

I had to do this school justice; I had to do these people justice.

Seemingly overnight, I had about 1,500 things on my plate, on top of all of the rest. We had to write stories on the dozens of events going on around the school, anything from a piece on the mountains of mail we received from schools around the country, to one on the survival of a student who was shot in the legs and had to run and hide for safety. The editors and I organized a new section of our website titled "MSD Strong" to funnel these stories. On top of that, we had to scrap the entirety of our third-quarter issue and start writing the memorial issue dedicated to the seventeen people we lost. An issue that usually would take eight weeks, we had to do in about three. I had to take pictures, and edit, and write three stories at once over and over again, not to mention my non-newspaper-related responsibilities.

Needless to say, I was drowning.

And still, I had yet to really address the emotions coursing through me. The day of the shooting, I cried the entire ride home with my mom, still reeling from my hours in the closet, not knowing if I was going to die. But after that? I think I just felt numb. I boxed away everything that I felt about the shooting, about the trauma, because the second that I let myself feel everything would be the second that I would become useless in this fight that we were working toward.

In relation to Newspaper, a similar self-destructive philosophy applied. Every journalist knows that when dealing with extremely emotional topics (like the murder of seventeen people), you need to compartmentalize and face some intense emotions. But when the topic is *yours*? When the topic is the murder of seventeen people you *know,* and the trauma is yours and your community's? When the topic is your friends and family? That emotion obviously grows tenfold.

Immediately, I had to interview victims of the shooting, many of them friends of mine, and hear their stories of watching their friends die around them. I listened to them and pretended like I didn't want to just sob uncontrollably.

It meant so much to me to write stories honoring the victims Alaina Petty and Joaquin Oliver for the memorial issue. Alaina was the sister of one of my close friends, someone I love so dearly. The process of interviewing their family, seeing them at their most vulnerable, yet still trying to maintain a level of professionalism and stoicism, was one of the hardest things for me to navigate and understand.

At the same time I was interviewing friends and family members in Parkland and other states for the memorial issue, journalists from all over the country also interviewed me. I had to listen to their misconstrued ideas of the weapon, event, and criminal that changed my life forever. These people had absolutely *no* idea what it was like to be us, and yet they all had opinions on what we should do and say, or how we should act. It was all overwhelming, to say the least.

For some background, I've always been a pretty sensitive person. Since childhood, loud noises, bright lights, and sudden touches all put me in a state of anxiety. And ever since the shooting, which provided me with the most intense sensory overload I had ever experienced, that anxiety had worsened. Loud noises didn't just make me uncomfortable; they petrified me. Sirens and alarms didn't just make me cringe; they put me in a state of unbearable panic.

And now, suddenly, every moment of my life was a form of sensory overload. My inner fear and pain and grief were battling with my need to interact with others every moment of the day while I was working to reach my goals of change and awareness.

So, like any teenager wholly unequipped to deal with the things I faced, I completely shut off. In order to accurately portray the lives of the victims in Newspaper, and to focus on effectively changing things in this country, I tried to put my emotions in a little box in my mind, locked away. Because, truthfully, how could I not? So many of my peers were trying to move on, trying to live their lives. But I was saturated in the events of February 14 and its aftermath every day. I was reading and writing stories about that day and the people we lost; I was researching the gun violence that affected me specifically. I saw people saying vile and terrible things about my friends and me, simply because we were fighting for what we believed in and writing about it.

How could I comprehend all of those feelings: my dead friends, my ruined childhood, my decimated relationships, my newfound purpose? My solution was to have no feelings at all. I didn't recognize what happened to me, let alone what happened to the people in the building on the same campus with me. Because the second that I did, I knew I would break. So I made sure that I didn't. And honestly, it made me more productive and more able to fully write and speak. By locking my feelings in a box I couldn't reach, I didn't have to deal with them, and I didn't have to hurt as much as I truly should have, feel as deeply as I deserved to, cry as hard as I wanted to.

Newspaper allowed me a place to release those emotions. I would have gone absolutely insane had I not had this outlet. Even though I was not addressing my feelings, I was writing and working and had found a purpose for myself to raise awareness about the plague that is gun violence.

It wasn't until the March For Our Lives that it actually hit me. Samantha Fuentes, a student who was shot on February 14, was speaking, and she explained how that day was Nicholas Dworet's birthday, one of the victims. I knew this fact, had seen it on Twitter, but when 800,000 people on Pennsylvania Avenue, participating in a march that was started by my friends, began singing "Happy Birthday" to my dead classmate, I realized how totally messed up this situation was. I started bawling, sobbing, crying harder than I think I ever had. I could barely breathe. I couldn't comprehend that I had been there that day, when seventeen people died. That it happened to them, to *me*. There was a part of me that was so confused: it had been a month since this happened, so surely I was over it.

But I had never really dealt with it in the first place. I had become so laser-focused on what I wanted to accomplish that my compartmentalization of my feelings forbade me from feeling at all. And here I was, standing with my camera at the March For Our Lives on Pennsylvania Avenue, my chest tight, my eyes squeezed shut, wailing to the song "Happy Birthday" in my friend's arms.

I suppose that's when grief hits you—when you least expect it.

That was when I realized that while it was important not to explode from all of the emotions inside, it was also important to deal with them in a healthy way. And, admittedly, healthy is not my forte. But I used Newspaper as an outlet. I used journalism as an outlet.

While writing has so many amazing purposes to help others, it can also be an avenue to help yourself process emotions and feelings. And self-care is something that I am still learning as I heal from February 14 and the days following. I am working hard every day not only to manage the pressures of being a journalist reporting such important stories, but also to manage the trauma that I have experienced, and the regular concerns of being the teenager that I still am.

FROM PARKLAND TO PENNSYLVANIA AVENUE

Putting Together a National Movement

by Delaney Tarr

The days of forming the March For Our Lives I remember the most fondly are the very first, when we all sat together on the floor of Cameron Kasky's living room. We had been brought together in different ways, some of us through friendships, others by chance. I was more on the side of chance. The day of the rally, where Emma, David, Cameron, and I gave our first speeches, was also my first day as a member of March For Our Lives. At the end of the rally, we were brought together for an interview on *CBS This Morning,* and after that, I was invited over to Cameron's house for some mysterious meeting.

Little did I know, I was at the start of an absolutely life-changing experience. The moment I walked into the room I was surrounded by around twenty passionate, shouting teens. It was overwhelming, of course. But it also held a certain level of excitement. There was hope in the air, something anyone could feel. Every other person was on the phone with some news organization, and many of us were already honing our message. We sat down to strategize, our open discussion often interrupted by near-constant calls from the media.

From there, the movement ballooned into something massive. Days later we announced the march in a day filled with interviews, every person splitting off to tackle their designated organization. We set up in the park next to the school and began spreading the message. It was strategic in a way, but it was also a complete disaster. We could barely keep track of each other, and that was before the general public showed up. Somehow word had gotten out about where we were, and our press conference turned into a political rally. Once crowds began to form, I think it became clear exactly how big the March For Our Lives could be.

It was hard for me at first. I had experience being on camera, but that was as a journalist and anchor on my school's news program. I was used to asking the questions, not answering them. As a reporter, it is in my blood to stay in the shadows and observe, not to parade out and be the story itself. Truth be told, reporting the story is a coping mechanism in a way. It adds a layer of distance between the writer and the subject, almost like a buffer.

But with the march, that level of distance was impossible. We were all in as soon as it began, and every waking moment soon became dedicated to the progression of the March For Our Lives.

Eating, sleeping, self-care, they all became things of the past. Now it was phone calls, messaging, and lots of stress. Lots of stress. Was it healthy? Probably not, but it was kind of necessary to organize what we did as quickly as we did.

Coordinating it all took an absurd amount of work. It was endless meetings in a variety of locations, filled with phone calls from different bigwigs who would help us organize and set up the actual march. But the core of the work, the outreach and spirit of the movement, was done among our little group.

We were the ones with a map hung up in our tiny office, each sibling march marked off in a growing mass of destinations. We were the ones sitting on a floor, or at a table, or on any piece of furniture possible. Maybe we weren't doing the nitty-gritty, like applying for permits, but we were the heart of the message, strategy, and outreach.

The planning wasn't always perfect, and there were plenty of arguments. We would bicker about small things, disagreements brought on by stress and exhaustion. Sometimes we would overwork ourselves. There were many unpleasant meetings where at least one person left unhappy. We were, after all, giving up our personal lives for the cause. We left behind our friendships, our extracurriculars, and spent every waking moment working on the march. Yet that's what happens when friends have to work together. A lot of what caused those fights is what made us work as a group.

We were often too passionate, a bit difficult to control. We would state our opinions and give speeches without rehearsing them or editing ourselves. We kept the message the same, but our statements were often shifting in the moment. Sure, it would make us upset with each other, but it also made us so effective to the outside world. Of course, we always made up. Whatever ill will we had would fade when we realized that stress was causing our anger toward each other. Then it was back to work.

As time progressed, our roles changed. Different members of the group had different responsibilities, but we all worked hard. The majority of my work lay in doing interviews with every out-let, from CNN to Fox News, and speaking at women's summits, as my skills seemed to be more focused on women empowerment. I would travel around the country and speak on panels full of powerful women to spread our message, fund-raise, and build support for the march.

In my free time, I had my pick of televised or print interviews to give, with the occasional opinion editorial to write. It seemed like this was the reality for most of us: talking to members of the media. We would be tossed on CNN, CBS, or even FOX, depend-ing on what our schedules allowed. Eventually, this all connected to our specific roles for the day of the march. Mine happened to be giving a speech.

The group had analyzed who had the most social impact, and we came to a consensus with the help of some outside input on who would get to speak. With the opportunity to speak came a whole new level of pressure. Before, I simply had to attend the march that I had dedicated the past month of my life to plan-ning. Now I had to actually speak to the hundreds of thousands of people we believed would come, with millions more watch-ing on every platform available. It was an unprecedented level of stress, but also one that we had grown accustomed to. Rather than anchoring the school news program that nobody really watched, I was speaking to nearly a million people.

Soon enough, the comfort of our quaint office was ripped away, both by death threats and stalkers who hung around outside, and by a quick change in location to the new home of the March For Our Lives: Washington, D.C. In our office for the days before the D.C. march, everything became about ten times as hectic. There was barely a free moment, with each one of us being shuffled off to a new interview every hour. The days leading up to the march were a blur, and I can only vaguely remember writing my speech the night before I had to walk onstage.

Yet, getting up onstage, and being there with all of those people, made all of the stress worth it. I may have blacked out the memory of giving my speech, but I can easily recognize March 24 as the best day of my life. Nothing is as satisfying as seeing hard work pay off, and that's what we all saw that day. From February 14 to March 24, we had one mission. And we not only achieved it—we far surpassed it. With over 800 sibling marches, and more than 800,000 people marching in D.C., the numbers were hard to ignore.

EXTRAORDINARY ACTS

Junior Lorenzo Prado Is Falsely Identified as a Suspect in Shooting

by Daniel Williams

When the fire alarm went off for the second time around 2:20 p.m. on February 14, junior Lorenzo Prado was in the auditorium sound booth working on lighting for Marjory Stoneman Douglas High School's upcoming musical production *Yo, Vikings!* Because it was so close to the end of the school day, he decided to finish fixing the lighting equipment, confident that the fire alarm was just a fluke.

As he continued working on the spotlight, Prado heard banging on the auditorium doors. He ran down the stairs and found around 75 students trying to get in. Prado learned that there was a Code Red issued and immediately ran back to the sound booth and closed the door behind him.

"Since I was the only one in there, I was the reason why so many people were able to hide in the auditorium," Prado said. "It's scary to think that if I would've left with my friends when the fire alarm went off, all those kids might not have been able to get in."

While in the booth, Prado texted his friends and family, trying to find out if the Code Red was real or a drill. Occasionally, he would look through the booth windows at the auditorium seats, where people were whispering and pointing at him. He tried to ignore them because the last thing he wanted was for people to think he had anything to do with the situation. But unfortunately, that is exactly what happened.

As Prado sat in the booth, the door kept rattling like someone was trying to get in. Thinking it was the shooter, he hid underneath the table, fearing for his life. But it was the SWAT team that came bursting in.

"At some point, the door started shaking. I was pretty freaked out because I thought it might've been the guy. I was so relieved when I heard multiple people because I knew it was the police," Prado said.

Prado got up from underneath the table, ready to evacuate the building, but to the law enforcement officers he was a suspect. When they reached the top of the stairs, Prado was ordered to get down and put his hands up. Startled and confused, Prado got on his knees and put his hands behind his back.

The SWAT team escorted Prado out of the booth, and when they reached the bottom of the stairs, he realized he had his phone in his hand. When he tried to put his phone into his pocket, the officers immediately reacted by stepping back and shouting at him to drop the phone. Prado had no choice but to drop it, shattering the screen and destroying the home button. He was then handcuffed and placed in the corner next to the girls' restroom, held at gunpoint.

"I was pretty scared. Although there was a woman guarding me with a gun and another officer near the doors, I could hear everything from their walkie-talkies and knew that they still did not know where the shooter was. That's how I found out why they were so suspicious of me," Prado said.

It turns out that Prado perfectly matched the description the officers were given of the shooter. He was wearing a maroon collared shirt and black pants, the same outfit the shooter wore that day. Prado was kept there for what felt like days, knowing that any sudden movements could end his life.

He was eventually uncuffed and allowed to call his mom, but was still detained. After the shooter was caught, Prado was released and went to evacuate the building. But as he passed the Freshman Building outside, he was grabbed by the neck and questioned extensively by law enforcement.

After providing detailed answers, Prado was finally able to leave the school grounds with his peers and reconnect with his friends who had initially evacuated during the fire alarm.

The following Tuesday, Prado rode a bus to the state capital along with his classmates to talk to legislators. He took to the podium and spoke about how it was not only the shooter's fault, but the fault of the law that allowed him to purchase a firearm "before he was able to drink beer."

"I heard talk about giving guns to teachers at school. We shouldn't solve our gun issue with more guns; it's like fighting fire with fire," Prado said. "These school shootings are a disease that is plaguing this country, and we need a cure before there are any more casualties."

PHOTOGRAPHING REVOLUTION
The Parkland March

by Josh Riemer

I carefully gripped my camera lens as I stood defiant in a swarming crowd of impassioned people, capturing the forefront of a revolution. My eyes were locked, as was my camera, on the passionate speakers who are so clearly the future of our country. I wanted to put my hands down and bask in the marvel of the events unfolding in front of me, but my camera came first. I slowly brought the viewfinder up to my face and snapped a few stills. I skimmed the crowd, filming and photographing the passion, the anger, the proud displays of a hurt community. My photos did not speak words; they shouted them. People came from coast to coast, as far as California, to protest and make clear their views and priorities. They came to be heard. Students and teachers alike stepped up on the stage, and they inspired everyone. They had fire in their eyes and compassion in their hearts. The crowd cheered for them. I cheered for them. I knew that was exactly what a revolution looked like. I stopped, putting my camera down, and I took everything in. Photography is my medium to inform, and on March 24, 2018, I had made up my mind that I was going to cover it all. I continued to document the speeches. A few hours passed. The speakers had finished, and it was time to march.

The swarm of protesters migrated to the front entrance of the park. I picked up my equipment, and I felt myself start to drift naturally in that direction. The entire intersection was blocked off, and crowds began to gather. A gust of wind broke me from my trance. I found the front of the march, where some of the movement's most influential speakers had gathered. I crouched down, with the thought that I might break into the area where the news stations and all the professional photographers were doing their job. Protesters were lined up as far as I could see.

After some instructions on where to go, we started marching. That day I must have tripped over at least ten news reporters, trying to get the photos that would give face to a revolution. The march was unlike anything I had ever seen. These people, who had gathered and marched together, were strangers to each other, but they were joined in a common objective: to incite change. We were hurt as a community. This home I knew as beautiful, tight-knit Parkland was torn apart at the seams, and we were putting it back together. We screamed out to the world, and the world was listening. I walked backward, steadily pointing my camera at the endless line of empowered parents, children, and teachers. I was overtaken by a level of pride the likes of which I had never felt before. The energy was pulsating through the crowd, and it was inescapable.

We then reached the school. As we began walking past Marjory Stoneman Douglas High School, the crowd fell silent. The revolution suddenly paused to recognize the gripping reality of what had happened at the school, the place where this revolution all began. A sea of heads turned toward the memorial: a sacred spot where loved ones, friends, and onlookers alike went to pay their respects and honor the fallen students and teachers. I got emotional. I put my camera down for a few moments and remembered how we got from mere thoughts and prayers to this. Activism. Then I picked my camera back up. I took some more stills. The group I was with turned around and started venturing back to the park. I watched the crowd behind us do the same. The students at the front of the march used the megaphone again. The crowd around me raised their collective heads and continued their first fight for justice.

The second part of the march was arguably more impactful than the first. This was where I got some of my best photos. The protest signs were held higher, and the chants for change were even louder. The megaphone emphasized our meaning, but the collective force of our voices was what really rang out through the trees. When you look at the pictures, you can almost hear what these people were shouting. The message was resonant. The crowd was marching more forcefully. I eventually started walking backward at a consistent pace, lifting my camera above the sea of heads and posters, snapping photos left and right. Protestors chanted "Who are we? MSD!" and "Show me what democracy looks like! This is what democracy looks like!" They cried out to the world to show that they were not messing around; this was not a fad, and their voices would not be silenced. They would be the ones to bring about change in this country, and maybe even the world.

For the first time in a long time, I felt that we as a people, young and old, were making a difference. I felt that finally, after all these years, the gears of democracy and bureaucracy were grinding, and the world would change for the better. I believe that everyone left that day with a sense of duty, but also one of accomplishment. I think we all went home with a certain peace of mind, because even though Parkland will be scarred forever, at least a positive change was birthed from our pain. I do not do what I do just for WMSD News. I do not do what I do just for myself, my friends, or even my family. I do what I do for everybody, because we as human beings need to sanctify these moments, and remember when we took strangers arm in arm and together stood up for what we believe in. We as humans have a responsibility to make our voices heard. Everyone has a story to tell, and everyone expresses themselves differently. Photos are how I express myself. These photos are my contribution to the revolution. A new day is coming, and until then, we're not going to stop documenting change, and we are certainly not going to stop marching.

THE MARCH FOR OUR LIVES, D.C.— COVERING HISTORY IN THE MAKING

Team Reporting

THE *EAGLE EYE* MEETS THE *GUARDIAN,* BY REBECCA SCHNEID

I hadn't always thought about journalism as a career. Yet, when I joined the *Eagle Eye,* especially after I saw our impact after the shooting, I knew that working at a newspaper or news company like the *Guardian* was something I dreamed of doing. But while I was so incredibly excited to work with the editors of a newspaper I had read since I was a kid, there was a problem—I was getting this opportunity because of such an awful thing.

Then the meeting in New York came almost exactly a month after the shooting, and everything changed. The editors at the *Guardian* reminded us of why we were doing this in the first place, to raise the voices of our peers and to fight for our friends. This opportunity was a privilege, but it was for a cause that was bigger than us.

The meeting consisted of about ten editors from the *Guardian* and twelve of our editors and staffers, and it was one of the most productive and thought-provoking meetings I have ever been in. We weren't a ploy for them to get more readers or silly children to them—we were real assets and partners in their mission to accurately report on the biggest story in the country. Since we were in the epicenter of the movement, we were uniquely qualified to report on it. And that feeling of partnership and camaraderie I felt as they listened to us as equals and we brainstormed like a team pushed me to take charge and really work to be the best reporter I could be.

We knew how busy we would be in the weeks leading up to the march, as we were finishing our memorial issue. So we agreed that their reporters would cover some important stories we wished we could write but knew we wouldn't have the time to do justice. They wrote a harrowing story about the choices teachers made on February 14 when locking their doors, published our manifesto on ending gun violence, and got us an interview with Senator Bernie Sanders (an opportunity that I will be forever grateful for). All of this was still in the weeks before the march.

The true strength and power of the *Guardian/Eagle Eye* team would be seen on March 24, when our reporting skills and their website led to an amazing result. Twelve of us were in the student section of the march and behind the stage, interviewing and taking pictures of speakers, students from MSD, students from inner-city schools in Washington, D.C., and Chicago, and celebrity supporters like Miley Cyrus and Ariana Grande. But none of these interviews and encounters from both those deeply affected by gun violence and those who supported our mission would have ever seen the light of day if it wasn't for the work of the *Guardian* to help us get it onto the internet.

Later, I had the amazing opportunity to work with the *Guardian* editors to write about my day at the March For Our Lives, one of the most emotional days of my life. Not only did it allow me to share how gun violence affects people everywhere, especially people of color, but it also allowed me to reflect on my experience and find some closure.

As an aspiring journalist, working with the *Guardian* was a dream come true, giving me a glimpse into the important, not-so-glamorous work of being a reporter and a contributor to the public flow of information. And their willingness to listen to us, no matter our age, and make our voices heard was inspiring.

Photo by Kevin Trejos

"I'm here for Joaquin. I'm here because no one should ever have to go through what we went through, what these parents went through. . . . We're here to change America, honestly."

—SAM ZEIF, MSD senior

SPEAKING OUT, BY CHRISTY MA

On the day we arrived in Washington, D.C., we were brought to the Newseum to learn about the First Amendment, the fundamental right Americans often take for granted, the right to freedom of speech. I was one of five students on the *Eagle Eye* staff chosen to speak onstage with Margaret Brennan, an American journalist and current moderator of *Face the Nation* on CBS News.

Before the panel began, my peers and I requested that the moderator refrain from bringing up the shooter himself, because the *Eagle Eye* staff had agreed that he did not deserve any media attention, even in a negative light. However, we were caught off guard when Brennan persisted with a question asking if we knew the shooter personally before Valentine's Day. Instead of going in-depth sharing our accounts of the shooter, we knew without saying a word to each other that we had to redirect the conversation toward the activism taking place at our very doorsteps and the process of reporting on such a dynamic movement. We were there to shed light on the American epidemic of gun violence and the actions taken to change the course of such an epidemic rather than give glory to the shooter.

After the panel, Mary Beth Tinker, a free-speech activist, approached us. We knew that Tinker had been an appellant in the landmark Supreme Court case *Tinker v. Des Moines,* which was a victory for free speech rights during the Vietnam War. Tinker told the *Eagle Eye* staff that our work has inspired her and reminded her of her activism as a teenage girl. When she was suspended from school for wearing an armband in protest of the Vietnam War, she and a few other students sued over the violation of their free-speech rights. The case went all the way to the Supreme Court, which ruled that her armband protest was protected under the First Amendment. The *Tinker* case was an important victory, establishing that student voices should not be suppressed. Although Tinker says that the *Eagle Eye* has inspired her, she has inspired us by setting an example of how persistent activism and freedom of speech can move a stagnant nation toward imperative change.

"[Whenever I see another school shooting on the news], it makes me angry. It makes me want to host a march on Washington, if I could do it all by myself, because people are forgetting."

—JACKSON MIDDLEMAN, who was in middle school in Newtown at the time of the Sandy Hook massacre

BIRD'S-EYE VIEW, BY SUZANNA BARNA

I was so grateful to be included on the team of *Eagle Eye* staff members who had the amazing opportunity to work with the *Guardian.* As a staff photographer, it was my mission to record

In the WMSD-TV classroom, the door between the computer workroom and the larger classroom stands ajar after the SWAT team clears the classroom on February 14, 2018. Students and TV Production teacher Eric Garner barricaded the door with a bookshelf as the shooting unfolded. *Photo by Eric Garner*

At the vigil held on February 15, 2018, at Pine Trails Park, MSD students, teachers, and parents gather with thousands of community members to mourn and remember the lives of the seventeen students and teachers killed the day before. *Photo by Kevin Trejos*

Students leave messages for their seventeen fallen Eagles at the vigil. *Photo by Kevin Trejos*

MSD senior Emma González (above) delivers her impassioned "We Call B.S." speech before hundreds of protesters on the steps of the federal courthouse (below) in Fort Lauderdale, Florida, three days after an armed gunman killed seventeen students and faculty at Marjory Stoneman Douglas High School. *Photos by Suzanna Barna*

The outside of Florida Speaker of the House Richard Corcoran's office after a group of MSD students and alumni were barred from speaking to him, despite having a planned private meeting. *Photo by Kevin Trejos*

Spectators sporting "We Call B.S." T-shirts watch from the gallery as the Florida House of Representatives holds a session on February 21, 2018. Less than a week after the tragedy, hundreds of MSD students traveled to Tallahassee to lobby Florida legislators for stricter gun laws and improved mental health laws. *Photo by Kevin Trejos*

Banners from all over the nation, filled with messages of support, encouragement, and love, line the hallways at MSD to welcome the students back to school just two weeks after the deadly shooting on Valentine's Day 2018. *Photo by Kevin Trejos*

AP Language and Composition teacher Laurie Edgar embraces and kisses a therapy dog visiting her classroom. Dozens of volunteers brought their licensed therapy dogs to MSD, many through the end of the school year. *Photo by Rain Valladares*

On March 14, 2018, the one-month anniversary of the deadly shooting, the entire school stands for seventeen minutes of silence during a planned walkout to the campus football field. Many students continued their walkout, leaving school in protest and walking to nearby Pine Trails Park. *Photo by Kevin Trejos*

Eagle Eye adviser Melissa Falkowski and staff meet with journalists from the *Guardian* at 10 p.m. on March 23, 2018, to plan coverage and reporting assignments for the march. *Photo by John Falkowski*

MSD juniors Alexa Zarem and Zak Kostzer film the From Broadway With Love benefit concert at the BB&T Center in Sunrise, Florida, on April 16. Proceeds from the concert were donated to victims, survivors, and Shine MSD, a student organization whose mission is to heal the Parkland community through the arts. *Photo by Eric Garner*

MOMENTS FROM THE
MARCH FOR OUR LIVES

March 24, 2018

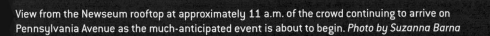

View from the Newseum rooftop at approximately 11 a.m. of the crowd continuing to arrive on Pennsylvania Avenue as the much-anticipated event is about to begin. *Photo by Suzanna Barna*

ALL SIGNS POINT TO CHANGE

Here is a sampling of some of the most clever and impactful signs spotted by our reporters covering the march.

After the official program concludes, Lewis Mizen, Richard Doan, Daniel Williams, Rebecca Schneid, Nyan Clarke, and Nikhita Nookala pose with an activist in a T. rex costume. *Photo by John Falkowski*

Brothers Ryan (MSD senior) and Matt (MSD alumnus) Deitsch embrace backstage following Ryan's speech about arming teachers with better pay and supplies instead of guns and arming students with knowledge. "We are done hiding. We are done being afraid. . . . It's time to fight for our lives," he said. *Photos by Kevin Trejos*

Eleven-year-old Christopher Underwood delivers a heartfelt speech about his experience witnessing the death of his teenage brother, who was shot and killed as he walked home from a graduation party. "I took my pain and anger and turned it into action," he said. *Photo by Kevin Trejos*

Ariana Grande, a native of Boca Raton, Florida, performs her hit song "Be Alright." Ten months earlier, a terrorist attack at Grande's concert in Manchester, England, left 22 dead. "This is for those brilliant students here today that are leading this march. . . . Thank you so much for fighting for change and for love and safety and for our future." *Photo by Kevin Trejos*

Left: Chicago students D'Angelo McDade and Alex King hold up their fists after delivering powerful speeches about how their community has been affected by gun violence, including McDade's impassioned plea for peace. "Violence cannot drive out violence, only peace can do that," he said. *Photo by Suzanna Barna*

Right: March organizer and MSD senior Emma González sheds a tear while leading an emotional 6 minutes and 20 seconds of silence, the duration of the gunman's rampage on February 14, 2018. *Photo by Suzanna Barna*

Hours before the march begins, *Eagle Eye* staffers and their adviser Melissa Falkowski hug, cry and laugh together in front of the March For Our Lives stage. Staffers embraced Falkowski when they noticed her crying, just as they were about to snap a group picture. *Photo by John Falkowski*

The nine-year-old granddaughter of Martin Luther King Jr., Yolanda Renee King, poses for a photo backstage with her parents, MSD junior Jaclyn Corin, and Parkland's Congressman Ted Deutch. "I have a dream that enough is enough. And that this should be a gun-free world, period," King said. *Photo by Kevin Trejos*

Protesters watch the March For Our Lives rally in an area adjacent to the main stage. Anticipating large crowds, organizers set up screens in overflow areas around Pennsylvania Avenue, allowing protesters to hear and see the program from multiple locations. Crowds extended at least one mile from the stage. *Photo by Chris Cahill*

Protesters line the streets to participate in the March For Our Lives rally. March organizers estimated 800,000 people attended the rally, which would make it the largest single-day protest in the history of the nation's capital. *Photo by Chris Cahill*

Jennifer Hudson, who lost her mother, brother, and nephew to gun violence in 2008, closes out the March For Our Lives rally with a performance of Bob Dylan's "The Times They Are a-Changin'." "We all came here for change today," Hudson told the crowd during her performance. "We're all here for a reason. We've all got a story; we've all got a purpose. And we all want change." *Photo by Suzanna Barna*

March For Our Lives speakers and organizers Edna Chavez, MSD senior Tyra Hemans, MSD junior John Barnitt, and MSD senior Diego Pfeiffer raise their fists in a show of solidarity, unity, and strength at the conclusion of the scheduled March For Our Lives program. *Photo by Suzanna Barna*

the march from our perspective—to take photos and pair them with quotes from crowd members and students so the *Guardian* could post it all on their live blog.

When I landed in the nation's capital the day before, I was already overwhelmed with a sense of history. I was in awe of the monuments that I had only seen in photos—the Lincoln Memorial, the Washington Monument—and it suddenly hit me. *My* school, in our unknown city of Parkland, had created a phenomenon larger than ourselves, out of something so indescribably evil.

The day of the march was exhilarating, exhausting, and also the most powerful of my life. As the *Eagle Eye* staff arrived at the march and finally entered at the correct press entrance, we peered upward at the stage before us with the beautiful view of the Capitol at its center. As we were about to take a picture together, we noticed our adviser, Mrs. Falkowski, overwhelmed with the significance of the moment, crying. There is a wonderful photo, taken by Mr. Falkowski, as we hugged, cried, and laughed together.

I had a unique experience as I was the only photographer to spend most of my time in front of the stage capturing the entire program. Positioned between the front row of student access and the stage, I stood among acclaimed journalists and security personnel as I took photos up close of the speakers, performers, and marchers. It was special access, and we were only allowed to have one representative in that area at a time.

As a journalist and student, I had unlimited access to the media tent and the blocked-off student section. I would go from talking with my friends to filming for a news crew to finding new crowd members to photograph. It was so surreal being interviewed and then having to excuse myself to go interview someone else.

A powerful moment for me was when I went to the nearby Newseum rooftop deck at about 11:00 a.m. and peered down at the crowds gathering down Pennsylvania Avenue toward the stage. Groups of people covered the asphalt, and all I could see were little heads. Later I learned that a tweet I sent to the *Guardian* and posted on my personal account received over a million views.

Through all the heartache that led up to the march, I felt nervous about the crowds and public safety and about how the speeches would impact the legacy of the MSD shooting. I had been so anxious up until the moment I realized that no matter what happened during the march lineup, the real hope lay with the crowds below me, full of individuals and groups from all over the country—not just Florida—who had decided that they'd had enough of gun violence and were ready to speak up. Participating and covering the march provided me with some sense of closure, hope, and empowerment that I will always remember.

Photo by Suzanna Barna

"Like I said, this is a generation where we are flourishing, and we are demanding. We're done living on assumptions, and now it's time to live on demands."

—EDNA CHAVEZ,
Los Angeles high school student who lost her brother, Ricardo, to gun violence

REPORTING FROM THE MEDIA TENT,
BY CHRISTY MA AND ZOE GORDON

Christy Ma

I was literally unable to see the end of the crowd on Pennsylvania Avenue, and being in front of it all, reporting and connecting with survivors of gun violence, was eye-opening and emotional. While we were all assigned to different spots and tasks on the day of the march, as cliché as it may sound, we were all together and on the same page.

I was assigned to the media tent with Zoe, a friend and fellow staff member, where the march organizers had reserved a spot for the *Eagle Eye*. I had the opportunity to talk to my MSD classmates who were speakers onstage, and meet students from cities like Chicago, Washington, D.C., and Los Angeles who had also faced gun violence, and in some cases had grown up with it. Although I realized that each person had their own unique experiences with gun violence, from witnessing family members at gunpoint to school massacres, it all ended the same way: being left to clean up the emotional and physical damage in the community. This vicious cycle of violence followed by government inaction was a common factor in each situation, and the students who spoke that day were just a few out of thousands who were tired of it. Reporting in D.C. gave me the ability to amplify those voices of pain, grief, and hope. This is what journalism is about, and this is why we will not stop.

"We were just so inspired by you guys, we said, what better thing to do in March than support you guys? That's really why we're here, we're here to listen to you—I'm so glad it's all students speaking, and we're here to listen to what you have to say and have your backs."

—LIN-MANUEL MIRANDA,
American composer, lyricist,
playwright, and performer

Zoe Gordon

Christy and I were selected to work in a special media tent for interviewing march speakers and special guests. We anticipated interviewing all the celebrities and speakers at the march. We wrote questions on our phones all night and planned how we were going to get pictures with Ariana Grande and Demi Lovato. Although we soon realized that not all of the speakers and celebrities were going to come through the press area for interviews, we still took in every second of the event.

I never expected the march to be fun, but it was so powerful, unfolding right in front of me in the most special way. All I could do was just take everything in.

One of the speakers said to raise your hand if you have been affected by gun violence, and when I looked out into the crowd, I saw thousands of hands go up. It made me realize that I'm not the only one who has been heartbroken by the loss of someone due to this issue. It also made me angry and drove home the need for this problem to be addressed immediately.

Though it seemed chaotic with so many people around me, it also felt welcoming because everyone was there to support the same agenda. I was there because I felt like it was my duty to honor the loss of my seventeen peers, and I believe we made them proud with all of our actions to support them.

"This moment, it affected me, because knowing that everyone from different backgrounds and from different parts of the country have come together to fight one problem . . . I have hope that change will come."

—ZION KELLY, Washington, D.C., high school student whose twin brother was a victim of gun violence

Photo by Suzanna Barna

BACKSTAGE AT THE MARCH, BY NIKHITA NOOKALA

My classmate Kevin and I discussed that if he was going backstage, he was going to get me there, too. We talked our way past security guards, with me ducking under taller people while he flashed his legitimate credentials. While Kevin was a journalist, like me, he was also one of the original organizers of the march and had all-access credentials that I didn't have. We hoped it would be enough, and with a lot of luck, I eventually got my own press pass. We got to talk to people I'd only ever seen on a TV or movie screen, like Lin-Manuel Miranda, Miley Cyrus, and Common, and young activists I'd never heard of before—from D.C., from Montgomery County, Maryland, and from Great Mills High School in Maryland, the site of the most recent school shooting at the time. It really was like watching history unfold seeing Yolanda King, the granddaughter of Martin Luther King Jr., standing next to my classmate Jackie Corin. And witnessing students like Zion Kelly and Edna Chavez, who had been surrounded by gun violence and had never gotten to have their voices heard, was incredibly inspiring and a reminder of why we started this movement in the first place. I got to see my best friend, Emma González, move hundreds of thousands of people to silence and tears at this huge event. It was all a whirlwind and one of the most memorable experiences I've ever had, not only as a journalist but as a student in America. It opened my eyes to how many voices there were out there, voices that I had never heard in my Parkland bubble.

It made me wonder if this was to be the legacy of Marjory Stoneman Douglas High School. Not the shooting, not the blood in the hallways, but the march. The voices. The memories. Is this to be the legacy of my alma mater? I can only hope so.

"To grow up in an environment where you see death constantly, it makes you want to see what you can do to better your community and better your situation. You all know that better than anyone."

—COMMON, rapper and activist

REPORTING FROM THE MSD STUDENT SECTION, BY BRIANNA FISHER

Going to the area where the march was held at 7 a.m., five hours before it actually started, made everything seem real. Looking at the stage and the reporters, along with the growing crowd that had also arrived early, I was still unaware of what I was about to go through. I would see a volunteer working at the march, checking in reporters at the press entrance, and just think, "Those people are working for my friends!"

The hours before the march allowed us to set up for the rest of the day. We started reporting immediately. From being interviewed to conducting interviews, the chaos of the day had only begun. We ran around from person to person, finding our favorite and most powerful signs and posters and interviewing their creators.

Some people were marching for a specific person, while others were marching for a school or community. Even seeing my camp friends who showed up for the march in D.C. from all over the country made me realize how far-reaching this topic was. It was surreal to see everyone fighting for the same reason.

I had the opportunity to interview Reverend Al Sharpton, the civil rights activist, who told us that he was inspired by us, which made me want to fight even harder to end gun violence. I also interviewed U.S. Senator Amy Klobuchar. Because she was a former prosecutor, she ramped up my motivation to help others and to continue with my dream to one day become a prosecutor myself.

Throughout the day, I was able to see the event through two lenses: as a student and as a journalist. It gave me a unique understanding because even though I was grieving alongside my friends, I still had the responsibility to report everything that was happening.

Photo by Nyan Clarke

"It's time to change Congress and start pushing in people that will make this change instead of the rhetoric. The politicians should remember that they work for us. The time is now."

—MARSHALL DAVIS,
parent of a Cypress Bay
High School student

REPORTING FROM THE CROWDS,
BY REBECCA SCHNEID

Since the shooting, my classmates have been working relentlessly, day and night, utilizing the March For Our Lives platform to make sure our voices get heard. We've gone on so many TV shows and been quoted in so many publications, it's hard to remember sometimes what our lives were like without it.

But at the march, it didn't take me long to realize how many different ways American lives have been devastated by gun violence. It's not just Parkland, and it's not just mass shootings. It's the streets of cities all around the country, communities that are plagued by gun violence daily yet do not have the same platform to speak about it as we do—whether because of their age, creed, color, or economic status.

In the crowd, I interviewed a mother who was carrying a sign that said "I survived gun violence, my daughter didn't." She told me she had been worried about her daughter's father's mental health and had tried to report her worries to the police. Nothing was done. Two weeks later, he killed her daughter. I heard so many stories similar to this one, each so moving and eye-opening.

I also talked to many students from Thurgood Marshall High School in Washington, D.C. These students have dealt with gun violence on their porches, in their gas stations, on the streets right outside their houses, places of worship, and theaters. They live in fear daily, but no one has listened to their roars as they pleaded for change.

It was humbling; it was upsetting. But it also reinvigorated my belief in the importance—no, the necessity—of this movement.

Gun violence disproportionately impacts people of color. It is our duty to make sure everyone can tell their story by sharing the platform we have received, in part due to our privilege.

I had a particularly touching encounter with those that had traveled from Newtown, Connecticut, the site of the Sandy Hook Elementary School shooting five years before. When you talk to people who have experienced the same trauma, you connect immediately with one another because you've been through something no one truly understands until they have faced it themselves.

The pain that fuels this passion for justice—you recognize it in other people. Their sympathy is genuine, wholly personal, and palpable.

We've seen the millions of people marching in the streets of D.C., Atlanta, Chicago, New York, San Francisco—even abroad. They have rallied behind us in a fashion I could never have even fathomed, and when the staff of the *Eagle Eye* arrived as the first Marjory Stoneman Douglas students on the scene, we immediately felt choked up as we watched the beginnings of a revolution form in this march.

I observed this diversity in the signs people brought to the march. One recited the names of the 17 fallen in my hometown, the 26 in Newtown, the 32 from Virginia Tech, and the 13 from Columbine. Another read "Which one is next?" Arrows surrounded it, pointing to the children around the poster, all potential victims of gun violence if the laws of our country do not change. Other signs chose to embrace a more humorous side, stating "We cannot fix stupid, but we can vote it out" and "You know this is serious when the introverts show up."

But I thought one sign encompassed what the rally was truly about. It read: "The times, they are a-changing."

And from what I saw at this march? I believe they are.

Photo by Richard Doan

"As far as growing up in Chicago, being a Chicago native, it's a lot of gun violence there. There are kids, there are babies getting shot. Coming from that background [and] losing a lot of friends and family [and seeing] today all the events happening around the nation with the students [shows] what the future needs. [These] educated individuals, they are being killed, so we wanted to come to support because not only do we have our own problems at home, but our kids are our home. Eventually these kids are going to grow up and make a difference, but they can't do that if they're killed in a classroom."

—DAVID BELL,
part of an organization that fixes homes for the less fortunate

EXTRAORDINARY ACTS

JROTC Students Help Shield Others Behind Kevlar Sheets Inside Classroom

by Ryan Lofurno

On February 14, as shots rang out at Marjory Stoneman Douglas High School, JROTC Captain Colton Haab and Captain Zackary Walls guided 60 to 70 students into a JROTC classroom. While inside, they shielded students with bulletproof Kevlar sheets in case the shooter came in.

"Zackary Walls, myself, and another JROTC student moved Kevlar sheets in front of everyone," Haab said. "The reason we did so was not only to give cover, but to also give the kids a sense of security and creating less visibility of the entire classroom as well as the people inside."

Kevlar is a strong material commonly used in bulletproof vests. The sheets inside the classroom were used as a backdrop for JROTC marksmanship practice. Luckily, these sheets were never needed to protect the students from the shooter. But Haab and Walls were prepared to fight back if the shooter entered the classroom.

"I went and found two- to four-inch pieces of wood and gave one to Zach. I tipped two wooden tables up and we waited. About a minute into me looking at the door, I realized there was a fire extinguisher sitting in the wall and had another JROTC student come and sit behind the table with Zach," Haab said. "My goal was if the door opened, I was going to swing and hit whatever was opening the door while the fire extinguisher would be deployed as a confusion."

Although the shooter did not go to their classroom, their quick thinking could have saved lives. This experience has changed Haab's perspective of life.

"It made me realize how life can change in a second. I was driving home from dinner [a couple weeks after the shooting] and there was a car accident that happened one-fourth of a mile in front of me and I stopped to check if everyone was okay and give whatever I could to try and help someone if there was something wrong, and Thank God there wasn't, but it just showed how everything can change so quickly," Haab said. "I've lost friends that I won't ever get to see again, and had the honor to lay to rest two of them."

INTERVIEWING BERNIE SANDERS

by Dara Rosen

On February 22, Jane Spencer, an editor from the *Guardian* newspaper, reached out to my adviser Melissa Falkowski to say how impressed she was with our website and offered to let us collaborate on their March For Our Lives coverage. In a meeting in New York with some of their journalists before the march, they asked us who we would like to interview as part of our partnership. The *Eagle Eye* editorial board gave a short list of names, including prominent Republican and Democratic politicians, one being Vermont Senator Bernie Sanders. A few days later, Mrs. Falkowski was told she could bring two students with her to Washington,

D.C., to interview Senator Sanders in person. She chose Rebecca
Schneid and me.

The *Guardian* arranged for all transportation, paid for our entire trip, and set up the interview with Mr. Sanders for eleven a.m.
on March 20. Mrs. Falkowski, Rebecca, and I were set to meet at
the airport on the morning of the interview at six a.m. for a flight
scheduled at 7:10 a.m. That flight was canceled due to inclem-
ent weather, so the *Guardian* booked us a flight with a layover in
Boston, and we didn't arrive in D.C. until noon, an hour after our
appointment. Luckily the senator had an opening in his schedule
later that day at five p.m.

Now we were in D.C. with nothing to do for four hours, so we
took advantage of that and did a little sightseeing. This being my
first time in D.C., I was amazed by all of the historical buildings
and landmarks. We went to the Library of Congress and were
given a private tour of the Capitol building.

At about 4:30, we walked to the senator's office and waited
for him to arrive. Rebecca and I were told that we would have
approximately ten minutes with the senator, so our list of questions would need to be small and focused. As we prepared, we
discussed which questions were the most important, which could
be cut or only used if we had extra time, what order the questions
should be asked in, and who would ask each question.

Rebecca and I debated which of us would have to ask the
hardest questions. We are both Bernie Sanders fans, so neither of
us wanted to seem combative or discourteous. In the end, we each
asked one of the difficult questions and were careful to be polite
and respectful.

Some of our hard-hitting questions included:

"Why did you vote against the Brady Bill in 1993, which would have introduced a lot of gun-control measures, including background checks and waiting periods?"

Answer: Well, there was a debate at that time. It was a long, long time ago, between what is now understood to be the case and that is kind of automatic background checks as opposed to a waiting time. And the people in my state preferred the automatic background checks rather than the waiting time.

"In 2006, you were awarded a C– rating from the NRA. What prompted that raise in rating?"

Answer: I have no idea. I have a D– lifetime average. The NRA is very arbitrary. In fact, if I'm not mistaken, I won't swear to you on this, you and you could cast exactly the same votes and you get a different rating. It is extremely arbitrary.

In our attempt to try to understand the events that took place at our school, we asked Senator Sanders:

"Your home state of Vermont is one of the most gun-friendly states in the nation, yet it has one of the lowest gun violence crime rates. Why do you think that is?"

Answer: In states like Vermont, which are very, very rural states, people hunt, people do target practice, people go to gun shows. Guns are a way of life and people take that very seriously, and they treat guns with a lot of respect. That is something very different in other parts of the country, where guns are used by people who are criminals, who are into drug dealing and so forth and so on. But I would also say—maybe I'm wrong on this, but I think I'm right—that in Vermont the vast majority of people, including gun owners, understand that we need what I call commonsense gun legislation.

We asked:

"Do you think that the NRA has the kind of hold on Congress the media portrays?"

Answer: It has a very significant hold. I think that hold may be breaking a little bit. You guys had some success in Florida.

We even asked him:

"Do you think President Trump has the courage to take on the NRA?"

Answer: No. President Trump lies all the time and he will come up with some ideas that may sound good. In fact, he had a televised meeting with some members of Congress and said all the things he wanted to do and two days later he backed away from it. No, I think he sees the NRA as very important to his reelection effort. And I do not think he has the courage to stand up to them.

The answers he gave to all of our questions were insightful and confident. He never stopped to weigh his words before he answered like most politicians do, and he didn't hesitate with his comments. Senator Sanders was straightforward and sincere with us, and he treated us like professional journalists.

When we asked him "Do you think Congress will pass any kind of legislation soon, and what obstacles do you think are in place to prevent that?" he answered immediately, "I think it is one hundred percent dependent upon grassroots activism."

We asked him a total of twelve questions that covered his

opinions on federal gun laws, grassroots movements, and the NRA. Some prompted lengthy answers, and others were short and to the point. The *Guardian* put together a three-minute video clip of the interview and posted all of the questions and answers in a transcript on their website that can be found at theguardian.com /us-news/2018/mar/23/bernie-sanders-gun-control-parkland -students.

Even though Senator Sanders was on a tight schedule, he made time to answer extra questions, and to take photos with us after the interview concluded.

Since the rescheduled interview took place after our original return flight left at 4:30 p.m., we had to book a later flight, which was canceled because of a coming snowstorm. The *Guardian* couldn't find any other flights out of D.C. that night, so we thought we were going to have to stay in a hotel. But thankfully Rebecca's dad is a miracle worker and found us a flight out of Baltimore. So we drove for an hour and a half to the Baltimore airport and finally arrived back in Florida around midnight.

Although this adventure took us through five airports in five different cities and on three different planes in only eighteen hours, I had the best twenty minutes of my life interviewing Bernie Sanders. I will be forever grateful to the *Guardian* for making this trip possible and to Mrs. Falkowski for choosing me to come with her to D.C. to conduct the interview.

PART TWO

MSD Strong

Photo by Suzanna Barna

TRAPPED

by Augustus Griffith Jr.

It was on February 14 when my classmates and I were sitting in my fourth-period study hall watching *Moana*. Without a valentine to share the day with, I was texting a fellow student about a bitter Valentine's Day rant I planned on sharing with the school's poetry club after school. It had been a somewhat peaceful, if uneventful, day, rife with the usual stress that came with schoolwork. At least for me. Some of my classmates, the thoughtful people they are, took the occasion as an opportunity to shower those closest to them with extravagant romantic displays. I both appreciated and resented the thought as I typed.

At some point during the movie, my history teacher, Mr. Nastasi, got up from his desk and stood in the doorway, questioning a student who had apparently run in from downstairs. I didn't think much of it. Minutes later, the fire alarm went off. Almost mechanically, I and twenty other students picked up our stuff and prepared to exit the building. Mr. Nastasi lowered the volume on the movie, turning on the lights as he continued to stand out in the doorway, consulting with other teachers as they tried to figure out what was going on. We'd already had a fire drill that day. He wouldn't let any of us leave the room. One visual that's been haunting to recall was the sight of a sea of students in the hallway, frantically running what I would later learn was the wrong way. The floor shook with their collective movement. A single loud bang emerged from the stairwell down the hall and resonated throughout the school, shaking our student body to its core. Suddenly, we all looked to Mr. Nastasi for reassurance as he calmly but firmly uttered the words that would change my life forever: "Get in the goddamn corner, now."

Our room was like the others in the Freshman Building. It was a relatively spacious area with a small metal door and a row of windows next to it. Our position in the hallway was quite possibly a lucky one. We were the farthest classroom from the stairwell the gunshot rang out from. The only room farther than us was a teacher planning room, which was right across from the second stairwell. Between it and our room were the bathrooms. Completely enveloped by adrenaline, we rushed into the too-small corner behind the teacher's desk, the only spot not clearly visible from outside the door. We all ducked as Mr. Nastasi rushed to shut off the lights and the now barely audible TV in an instant.

He shoved his heavy wooden desk in front of the door and joined us, sitting and making sure we were all compacted. The bangs grew nearer, and louder, and faster. We heard screams. We heard cries and pleas. Silencing them with an unmatched volume and intensity, gunshots. They were right outside our door.

We ducked. The succession of the shots grew quicker and quicker. Was there more than one gun firing? We weren't listening, but we heard everything: every gunshot, every scream, every body thudding lifelessly to the floor. The fire alarm continued for minutes that felt like hours, though our eyes were fixated on the door in sheer horror. We were trapped and truly helpless, the shots eventually descending down the stairs, leaving us with only a terrifying, vague idea of what was going on and praying that no one would approach the door. A student screamed outside. He was pleading for help and sanctuary. I'll never forget his pleas.

The shots stopped eventually, introducing us to a piercing silence, soon followed by wailing sirens outside. The student in the hallway was still begging to be saved. We looked at each other somberly, unsure who it was and aware that we could do nothing. He knocked on our door, still screaming for help. He continued to desperately attempt to open the locked door, knocking gravely and loudly. Our teacher silently shook his head, reminding us not to open the door. Terrified, our eyes never drifted from the door, and we could do nothing but fear.

We were sitting ducks, frightened and helpless, for two and a half hours, but I felt like we had been stuck in that corner for days. Our reactions ranged from stone-cold denial to full-on panic and tears. We weren't soldiers. We were teenagers. I remember fearing that something had happened to my creative writing teacher, whose classroom was right next to the stairwell where the shots came from. This wasn't happening; it couldn't be happening. I quietly cried bitter tears as the fearful thought ran through my mind that I would never see my seven-year-old sister again. I stared at the door angrily, anticipating our demise. It couldn't happen here, I thought. Not like this. I wiped my nose on my sleeve so I wouldn't breathe too loudly. I was wearing a jacket with pockets that day, and inside my right one, I had a small planner for writing jokes. At some point during the silence, I took it out and placed it on the floor for fear of being mistaken for one of the people who had done this, purely because of the way the planner protruded out of the front of my jacket, appearing almost gun-like.

I don't remember exactly when the police arrived at our floor. Before they did, the student outside had been yelling to them downstairs, and I could no longer hear his screams. When they approached, I heard their radios and the officers speaking. The context of the sentence could not be understood, but the words "check" and "bodies" could clearly be heard. They evacuated the room across from us first. "Broward Sheriff's Office! Open up." It took several minutes, but it sounded like the people in the other room complied. Piercing screams interrupted the police chatter. And footsteps. The cries of my fellow students across the hall will never leave me. I couldn't fathom what they were seeing to trigger this extreme reaction—until it was our turn to leave the room eight minutes later.

We heard yelling, followed by knocking on our door. "BSO. Open up." A couple of people started to stand up, but Mr. Nastasi once again gestured for us to stay seated. The combination of my teacher's noncompliance and the screams from those evacuated first led me to believe that whoever was in the hallway was about to kill us. They knocked again: "Broward Sheriff's Office! Open up." Another officer suggested that our classroom may be empty. The one at the door rejected the idea, stating that he could see a girl sticking out of our too-small corner. Even when discovered, Mr. Nastasi, a genuine trouper, refused to open the door for them by staying silent, and we did the same. They had to break the window on our door and turn the handle from the inside. Once they came through, one officer stepped half inside and another was on the side of the door frame, his large weapon trained on us, ordering us to put our hands in the air. They asked us if anyone was injured. We weren't. If we had firearms. We didn't. They told us to stand up and form a straight line, putting our hands on the shoulders of the person in front of us. Mr. Nastasi asked if he could grab his keys off his desk. They obliged, letting him take his keys and then stand behind us. I left my phone on my desk in the chaos. I was too preoccupied with the fear of what lay outside our closed door to even think to ask about going to get it.

The first thing I noticed when we stepped outside was how bright it was. We had been skulking fearfully in the dark corner for at least two and a half hours. Nothing but a faint blue light from the windows in the back gave us light. It was . . . foggy. Was that smoke? I've never had a great memory, but I can recall each detail we saw in that hallway during our escape. None of us were looking, but we saw everything. It was carnage. There were bullet holes everywhere. Blood covered and stained the floor, and all of us got blood on our shoes. There was a girl lying facedown in front of the girls' bathroom, right next to our door.

I'd vaguely remembered the restrooms on the floor being locked when I went to use them earlier that morning. We turned, and I caught a glimpse of Scott Beigel, a geography teacher, down the hallway. He wasn't moving, either. Students lying near the elevators. We walked into the stairwell. At the top of the stairs, there was another body. I remember thinking it seemed like someone had dropped their belongings in an attempt to move faster. Black backpack, red phone case. As we moved down the stairs, I remember feeling relieved, in a sense, because when we were past the carnage, there was a temporary peace in the stairwell. Then we reached the ground floor. We exited the building from the side, and there was a bloodstain on the ground in front of the door, and more police officers than I had ever seen were standing in front of the building. Illusion shattered.

My classmates and I left the building shaking. I was a broken record once we crossed Holmberg Road to reach safety. It didn't feel like safety. I thoughtlessly repeated the same three words to myself as I broke down crying: "Those were students." When we'd exited the building, we were told to hold our hands above our heads to show that we weren't threats. I held my hands above my head long after we'd crossed the street, and only put them down when I realized I was the only person still keeping them up. The police were yelling at our line of students, asking if any of us had social media accounts or any pictures of Nikolas Cruz. I remember that name not making any sense. No human being could be responsible for what I'd just seen. This was the work of a monster.

We were crowded on the sidewalk opposite the school. I made a mental note of the people I knew were safe. I hugged strangers.

I searched desperately for friends, and I checked in with them by text, too. We were all crying. A friend of mine had seen a bullet in his classmate's head. A lot of the interactions after that one became a blur. Having left my phone on my desk, I texted my parents from a friend's phone, and my dad picked me up from the side of the road about an hour later. When I got home, I lamented, feeling responsible for the fact that my friends thought I might be injured because they could not reach me on my phone. I emailed those I could and then sobbed, staring up at the ceiling for hours. I was physically exhausted, but I couldn't close my eyes without hearing the screams. I'd hugged my family an inordinate number of times and told my sister that I will always, always love her.

The great debt we students owe to those we lost is difficult to repay: to always honor their memory and to fight for change. I remember the last time I spoke to Peter, one of the students who died that day. I have fond memories of Gina, having sat next to her in fifth-period geometry for about half the year. She was easily the brightest person in the room. The trauma is going to remain part of all 3,300 students who were there that day, forever. We walked out of Marjory Stoneman Douglas High forever changed. The students of Douglas are now brimming with tragic insight, a small community learning the meaning of loss and pain. A knowledge that will stick with us, all of us, even after the cameras leave.

Photo by Delaney Tarr

A NIGHTMARE INVADES MY REALITY

by Andy Pedroza

Wednesday morning rolled onto me like the day before and the day before that. Valentine's Day perfumed the environment around Marjory Stoneman Douglas. Carnations darted back and forth. Pictures with loved ones were taken every few seconds. A friend of mine, Emma González, handed me a bouquet of leaves. She knows I enjoy random things and I always gush about weird presents like that. My day was like any other day at school: people stressing out about AP courses, students fighting the behemoth of sleep in their classes. Everything was normal. Between third and fourth period, I walked halfway to the Freshman Building (where my algebra class was held) and talked to a friend of mine. I expected the typical chat but was surprised by a "Would you be my valentine?" That was pretty cool.

I strolled at a moderate pace—or "ran," as my classmates would call it—up the stairs into my algebra class. Because I'm an IEP student—meaning that I can test in a separate room for algebra—I took my test elsewhere and began the walk of doom back to class. Before returning, I strolled over to my support facilitator's room on the second floor of the main building. The room stood behind the main staircase that feeds into the Freshman Building, senior lot, and chemistry building.

I exchanged some words with my support facilitator. I left her room at about 2:20 p.m. I didn't hear much besides her air-conditioning system, but that changed as I started trekking down the stairs and back to the Freshman Building. Popping sounds, like those of a balloon bursting, erupted seemingly behind the building. I didn't think much of it. I guessed that it might have been a car tire blowing out or JROTC doing marksman practice or something. I was almost there, walking toward the doors of the building when the ricochets branded my ears with fear.

I didn't know what possessed me to do it, but I bolted into the building. I thrust the crimson metal door open and charged into the staircase to my right. I sprinted up the stairs at the same time the fire alarm began to blare. I knew exactly what to do. My school had enacted numerous security measures the month prior. Teachers were told to always keep their doors locked and not allow any students in if such a situation was to arise. All of my teachers told us that if there was ever a Code Red and a student wasn't in a classroom, the student would have to run to the bathroom and stand on the toilet. I made it to the second floor of the building, where my algebra class was held. For half a second, my vision darted from a classroom on my right to the bathroom ten feet in front of me. Gunpowder choked the hallway into submission.

I sprinted to the boys' bathroom and charged for the largest stall. I set one foot on the toilet—it was too slippery and would make too much noise. I decided that I should sit still behind the stall door and hope that the shooter wouldn't find me. I heard everything. I could only hope that the noise was coming from thirty textbooks being dropped at the same time—each one closer to the bathroom. I didn't know where the shots were coming from. I didn't know if the shooter was in the hallway right outside the bathroom or on the third floor above me. I didn't know if death would follow me to the stall. I didn't know anything. I was completely in the dark. I didn't know if these would be the last minutes I would spend on Earth. I thought about what death was like. I didn't know if I'd be mercilessly shot and killed in the bathroom. I didn't know if my parents would have to view the corpse of their son at a funeral. I didn't know if that morning would be the last time they'd see me. At 2:28 p.m., I texted my loved ones, telling them, "I just want to let you know I love you." My fingers trembled like glass in an earthquake. My heart punched and kicked and tossed around in my chest. I felt like it could burst out onto the wall in front of me. I had to tame my breath because I needed to remain absolutely silent; I took quick, concise breaths and exhaled accordingly. After a minute or so, I was able to stay quiet. My sister texted me back wondering if I was okay. She jokingly asked me if I was having a Valentine's Day breakdown, since it was very out of character for me to tell her I loved her. At 2:30, I answered her, saying, "There is a shooting right now. . . . Please call the police." Almost instantly, she texted back.

2:30 "Where are you?"

2:31 "Douglas."

2:32 "Are you safe?"

2:32 "I thought it was a drill but it's real."

2:32 "Tell me where exactly you are and who you're with."

2:33 "I'm by myself."

2:34 "Are you in a stall? I just called Dad. He's calling."

2:37 "I am."

2:37 "Please don't stop texting me."

I don't remember when I stopped hearing the gunshots. All I knew was that someone could still be in the building or the shooter or shooters could have migrated to a different part of campus. My father called me while I was still in the bathroom. The barely audible words dribbling out of my mouth affirmed that now was not a good time to talk.

I heard the police sirens; fear lifted its cold hand from my shoulder. I heard them pulling into the senior lot. Their radios echoed throughout the building. They entered the first floor, and I could hear them saying, "Where did he go?" I don't know how long it was until I heard them charging up the stairs. They were in the hallway outside the bathroom, and I could hear them loud and clear. I heard the bathroom door swing open. I saw bulbs of light paint the room. I immediately yelled that I was in the stall. I gingerly opened the bathroom door with my hands far above my head. They patted me down and instructed me to run outside. In shock, I asked them if I could pick up my backpack and bring it with me. They ordered me to leave the bathroom. I was in the hallway when one of them barked at another to escort me downstairs. We both ran down to the first floor. I opened the door leading out of the staircase, and at the bottom left corner of my eye, I saw Coach Feis's body on the ground. The police who escorted me out told me to "book it" over to the road that connects with Westglades Middle School.

Once I left the parking lot, I saw that the road was heavily coated by law enforcement. I fished my phone out of my pocket and called my sister. She picked up in half a second. Her voice drowned under her cries. I continued to assure her that I was okay—that I was outside of the building. I told her everything would be all right. I told her to think about where she was, that she was outside, safe, and to breathe in and out. I was ordered to hide behind a white SUV. A police officer patted me down and told me to sit behind the car. There were two girls next to me. One was standing up and talking on the phone. The other girl seemed to be hyperventilating on the ground. I looked over to her and said, "Hey, feel the grass beneath you. Look to the sky—look to the clouds. Breathe in this air. You will be okay. You are right here and not back there." I don't know what weight my words had, but I hope it helped alleviate her pain at least marginally. My father called me and told me that he was at the Walmart one minute away from Westglades. One of the officers walking by allowed me to see my father.

My dad and I talked as we walked over to his car. On the way, I saw my history teacher from junior year, Mr. Pittman, and asked him if his class was fine. He said, "Everything that happened was in the Freshman Building," precisely where I was. I have a friend in his class, so I called her. She was not in the best state. I said that I was fine, and I advised her to keep her hand over her heart and feel her heartbeat. I told her that if she felt it, she'd know that she was okay and that she was still here.

My father and I drove to our house. I saw my family friend and her mother. They asked me about what happened. After at least twenty minutes, I went to my kitchen to attempt to have lunch. My friend sat next to me, slowly chewing her lunch. The instinct to make her laugh kicked in. I had to make her feel okay; it was the only thing I could think of doing. She rose from her seat and took her dish to rinse it in the sink, precisely when my memory returned. Everything rushed back at me like numerous tsunamis and earthquakes hitting at the same time. The gunshots. The gunpowder. Hiding in the bathroom on the second floor of the building. Everything. The thoughts about death. Seeing Feis's body. Not knowing where the shooter was. Everything.

I did what I typically do when I want to let everything out: listen to Bob Marley and Phil Collins. I went on YouTube to search up "Three Little Birds" as I trembled and breathed haphazardly. I felt like a Chihuahua in a thunderstorm. I moved on to "You'll Be in My Heart," and everything I felt in the past hour came flooding out. My vision was obscured by my tears. My family friend escorted me to my bedroom. I asked her to leave me alone.

In that first week, my dreams were infected by my experience on the fourteenth. I was depressed and somber those first couple of days. I was engulfed in absolute sadness at the vigil. I could not control my tears when I saw the seventeen angels on the stage. I made sure to buy some nice things to put by their names. I remembered the times Joaquin made me laugh. I remembered when Nick Dworet presented a letter he wrote to his girlfriend in Creative Writing. I remembered seeing Feis in his golf cart every afternoon. I remembered speaking to Meadow back in freshman year. It was difficult for me, but I was able to heal and push forward. I watched comedy specials. I hung out with some friends. I went to the movie theater to watch some newer films. I shared elation with my TV Production family over inside jokes and new projects. I was able to get through by doing things I relished: videography, writing, telling jokes, and just flat-out laughing with friends. Doing all of that has made the chains of trauma around my ankles slowly deteriorate.

What happened on the fourteenth has made my school some creature with seven eyes and three legs. Everyone is paying attention to us. We are under an electron microscope. To those people covering our trivial events, please let us breathe. Please cover actual events, not just the things we normally do at school. Please cover stories that are not simply "Stoneman Douglas seniors are going to prom," "Stoneman Douglas band won an award," or "It's David Hogg's 18th birthday." Parkland is a community that has experienced an unspeakable tragedy. Please focus your cameras and your pens on Flint, Michigan, James Shaw Jr., the Dakota Access Pipeline, gun control, and other stories that need to be in the forefront of the media. We thank everyone for their support, and we greatly appreciate what you've done for our community. But we are students and teachers recovering from a tragedy—we are not creatures you can point at and stare down.

I am positive, I am passionate, and I am proud to be a Marjory Stoneman Douglas Eagle.

EXTRAORDINARY ACTS

Freshman Jason Snytte Saved His Classmates by Shutting His Class Door

by Brianna Fisher

Freshman Jason Snytte had no idea he would be deemed a hero when he ran to make sure his classroom door was closed. He was in English class in the Freshman Building during the shooting when another student exited the classroom to use the bathroom, and they heard shots in the hallway.

"I immediately ran to the door to close it once we heard the gunshots," Snytte said. "I wasn't sure if it was real or a drill, but I needed to make sure that we were safe."

Snytte's classmates were in shock when he ran over to the door. Nobody had time to process what was going on, let alone get up and close the door.

"Not in the moment did it even cross my mind to do what Jason did," freshman Michael Catapano said. "I thought Jason was brave for closing the door and shutting the lights."

At the time, Snytte did not realize the significance of his action. "I was kind of calm because we thought it was a drill," Snytte said. "Once I heard screaming and everything, I panicked and started texting my family and everyone to let them know I was okay."

Throughout the rest of the incident, Snytte felt that his class followed the directions for the situation of an active shooter almost perfectly. Everyone tried to remain calm and stay safe so that nothing happened to Snytte's class.

"My class mostly did everything right. That's why we were skipped over," Snytte said. "We just closed the door and the lights and made sure everyone was out of sight."

Days later, Snytte reflected on his role in the safety of his class and realized how he affected the lives of his classmates.

"Yes, this has changed me as a person," Snytte said. "It changes everyone, I'm assuming, and everyone should be different now and just appreciate things more. People should value life more for the people that were lost."

Snytte still does not deem his action of closing the door heroic—he said it was just the necessary thing to do in that moment.

"I would not use the word 'hero' to describe myself," Snytte said. "Others lost their lives saving people, like Coach Feis, and I just closed the door. I saved my own life and my class's once the shooter had passed over the room."

But people were still grateful for his actions.

"I would want to thank Jason for being brave and keeping us all safe," Catapano said.

THROUGH NEW EYES
From Student to Photojournalist

by Kevin Trejos

I've been a photographer for four years, and while I had experience working on photo shoots, I never put my hobby to a practical use. When I joined the *Eagle Eye* staff, I began to take many photos for the publication. I found photojournalism to be a useful and expressive tool for me to contribute to my journalism class and to visually represent the articles we published. It also let me use my hobby in school.

Usually the most riveting photojournalism I do is taking photos of events during spirit week or capturing a football or volleyball game for the school, but since the tragedy, I've captured some of my most powerful and memorable photos. I feel that through covering this tragedy as a student journalist, I discovered true photojournalism. These photos not only captured a physical location, but also conveyed the emotions and feelings around that moment. Photos could illustrate the process of grief and recovery that many students had to endure after the shooting and display the shift from hopelessness to embracing advocacy as students spoke out against the terror they experienced.

I've documented all I could since the shooting.

Even though I didn't have my DSLR camera on the day of the shooting like I usually do, I tried to take a couple of photos inside the closet I hid in. After we were evacuated from the school, I took photos of all the police and news media that had surrounded the school. It felt like I had a responsibility to record everything. I knew the documentation of any sort may be helpful for studying the tragedy in the future; it was the natural photographer and journalist in me to capture the world in pictures.

It was weird. That first day, I was unable to experience emotion, only shock. The noise and craziness of it all consumed me as I tried to get as much information as possible about what happened to my friends and classmates. My eyes stayed glued to news and social media throughout the night as I wished for more information and the safety of my peers.

In the days following, I was burdened with the task of photographing sensitive events like the vigils. Mrs. Falkowski asked me if I felt comfortable taking photos at the vigil, and although I agreed, I worried about blending in with the rest of the media and invading the privacy of my community. I made sure to carefully photograph the vigils, focusing on planned occurrences like Ted Deutch speaking and the speeches at the memorial service in the evening. Luckily, at the afternoon vigil where only Stoneman Douglas students and staff came to mourn and reunite, many media outlets did not show up. I was left to the task of photographing the event, although with the heavy emotions and conversations, I took only a few during this portion. In the evening, I took more photos, yet instead of crowding the stage and knocking over community members, I kept to myself and tried to take some of the stage from my location. Afterward I got photos of the angels and memorial items placed on the amphitheater stage. These photos were difficult, as I had to balance taking photos as a journalist and respecting people's privacy, avoiding exploiting them at their weakest.

One photograph that stands out to me especially was a long exposure I took two days after the shooting, when I first decided to return to the school. I've always enjoyed landscape photography, and this photo still gives me chills. It was ten p.m., and the street was dark apart from the police sirens and media tents that illuminated the school. I propped up my tripod underneath the Sawgrass underpass and took a photo of the scene in a wide-angle view. The lights are like the hope that people from across the country provided with their support for the Parkland community. The result was a perfect capture of the chaos of the weeks after the shooting.

I also took photos when students went to Tallahassee to advocate for changes in the state legislature before the session ended, and at many city events.

Photography gives me an outlet to report on the world around me. It gave me a way to document the events for my own memories, and also for the world watching our school and community. Photography and journalism let me separate from the heartache and focus on creating something from the destruction we endured.

EULOGIZING FRIENDS AND COVERING TRAGEDY

by Nikhita Nookala

Other journalists have told me that covering death and tragedy is the hardest part about the job. For me, this was part of my very first year of journalism. The last article I had written was an app review that we submitted for a contest. The next challenge I took on was covering the mass shooting that had killed seventeen people, including someone I had known for a long time, and the vigil that followed, which made me cry for hours.

One of the few rules we had in Newspaper was that you couldn't write about an event you were involved in because of conflicts of interest. But who on the staff didn't have a conflict of interest now? Everyone was there that day, and everyone knew at least one person on the casualty list. So it came down to who responded to the message Mrs. Falkowski sent out.

"Today I have to ask you to do something that will be incredibly difficult. There will be a candlelight vigil today and we need to cover it. We have a responsibility as journalists to tell the story of what happened and the stories of those who have passed or were injured. No one can tell their stories better than we can."

It took time to gather ourselves enough to put out those first two stories. Then we had to do the memorial issue. That was the most difficult project I have ever worked on. Everyone had to take breaks to pause and reflect on what exactly we were doing. We were profiling people we had passed every day in the hallways, adults who we had seen riding across campus on golf carts for our four years at Douglas, classmates we had sat next to for years.

For me, it was, and still is, difficult to accept that these people were gone. My mind kept holding on to the expectation that Carmen would stroll into class one day and call me crazy for thinking she would never come back, that all of it was just an insane, nightmarish daydream. But it never turned out that way, and at the end of each day—almost every day for a couple of weeks—I found myself in the newspaper room, sitting in front of monitors displaying two-page spreads filled with pictures of people I had never known, people I knew well, and people I'd seen in passing.

Covering death in journalism is one of the most challenging things to do, especially when the event that caused it is intertwined with some of the most polarizing political issues of the century. There are so many factors and people to consider. For example, freshman Peter Wang was a hero in death, holding the door open for other students. But should we include that in his profile? Was it more important to show who people were in life, or how they showed courage in their final moments? What was appropriate to share about their lives?

All of these questions ran through our heads with every word we wrote. As the deadline approached, it became apparent that the quality of the stories varied, and we needed them all to be powerful and moving. So the senior writers began to help the younger ones. They helped turn a list of facts about a person—favorite food, favorite movie, favorite book—into a meaningful paragraph about who that person was, what they valued, what they aspired to be, what they would have done, and what they already had done.

When covering death, we always have to remember the surviving family. We tried to include them as much as we could, but it became difficult when the family didn't want to be too public or wasn't able to talk about it, all understandable parts of recovery from trauma. But it became frustrating when we didn't have the information we needed to capture who a person really was. We desperately wanted the same quality of profile for each person, and it became difficult to do, especially when the student was in their first year of high school, like so many of the victims were. Most teachers didn't know them, only one grade of students really knew them, and they haven't been given many opportunities to make a huge impact yet.

Our school had dealt with this before, on a much smaller scale. Two students in the senior class had died over the last three years, and the *Eagle Eye* had written tributes to both. But most of the kids in Newspaper hadn't worked on those issues, and none of the current newspaper staff had ever written a 1,300-word profile on a student they knew. This was a whole new undertaking, and no one was sure that they were ready.

It was important to keep the political debate out of these stories and out of the news stories that were released just following the shooting. We owed it to the community to put out unbiased content, with respect for the victims, their families, and the community. Others were not so kind. There were people from the Parkland community protesting for and against gun control at the vigil itself. I wondered how people could do something so destructive at an event meant for unity.

Every time I was assigned to a story that had to do with the shooting, or an event for a memorial foundation, or a story about the support we were getting from the community, thoughts of my friend Carmen Schentrup ran through my head. I think it will take a long time to come to terms with the fact that a girl I was talking to at 1:00 p.m. was dead at 2:30 p.m.

There's a time and place for political talk, but memorials and news stories regarding death and tragedy aren't the place. That's a different headline entirely.

BALANCING GUILT WITH OPPORTUNITIES

by Carly Novell

When we were given the opportunity to write this book, I struggled with the idea—like I do with every opportunity I have been given in the aftermath of my school's shooting—because seventeen people had to die for us to have this platform. It feels unfair that seventeen voices were taken away for ours to be amplified.

The guilt that I've felt since the shooting is different from the typical survivor's guilt, where one wishes they died instead of the victims. My guilt overshadows every waking moment. Any time I feel happy, I remember what I, and 3,300 other students, went through on February 14. The few moments when I am not thinking about my school, my community, or my loss, I feel like I am forgetting the pain that my community has experienced since that afternoon. I try to reassure myself that there is nothing wrong with feeling okay at some points, but it's hard to convince myself of something I don't believe. Since the shooting, it seems that every moment of "happiness" is just my attempt to ignore my pain for a moment.

So when my dream of being featured in *Time* magazine was fulfilled, or when Hillary Clinton tweeted me, I couldn't help but recognize that both of these seemingly positive events were the result of the most horrific tragedy one can conceive. On top of that, I was being showered with praise and support due to my sudden relevance, but the shooting could have happened anyplace; every aspect was random. The attack on our school opened our eyes to gun violence, leading many of us to speak out. And the media attention we've received gave us a bigger platform to effect change. But there were so many other students all over the country who had already been doing so much more because of their long-held beliefs, not because they had been personally impacted by this issue—and I think they deserve more attention. So it was difficult for me to understand and accept people saying that I inspired them when all I did was tweet my opinion.

Although the catalyst for all of this was my school's shooting, resulting in the death of seventeen wonderful people, we as students decided to set a goal of making sure that no more people were killed, instead of becoming paralyzed by the fact that seventeen souls were lost. What matters is not how I got these opportunities, but the fact that I did get them, and that I am alive to receive them. Letting chances to strengthen my future pass me by because of what I went through wouldn't do the victims justice. The best way to honor them is to make the best future I can, even though they may not be in it.

So things such as participating in writing this book, or submitting my writing to *Time,* is using my experience to make a statement, but I am not using others' pain for my benefit. But things like meeting celebrities or receiving money from the victims' fund, for me—someone who wasn't even in the building—do not feel appropriate. I don't want to be handed things out of pity, or to take advantage of someone's agony or misfortune. I just want us to be recognized for our efforts and feel needed in the march toward change.

This line is often blurred, like when I got to meet Dwyane Wade. I was given the opportunity to write a story on his visit to our school, but at first I wondered whether he had come out of pity or awe. Writing the story made me feel passionate and hopeful again for the first time in so long, but I felt awful because Wade was connected to our school through Joaquin Oliver, who was buried in Wade's jersey. Dwayne Wade did not visit our school to talk to student journalists—he came to grieve alongside students. I couldn't tell which one I was in that moment. Regardless of why he came, it was a great experience and we have to accept the offers that come our way. I am not going to let a single moment keep me from having a successful future. I can't let life pass by because of a tragedy that I cannot reverse.

So accept the opportunities that come your way, and don't forget to extend them to others as well. There must be a mutual benefit. The difference between accepting an opportunity and taking advantage of one lies in the way one benefits from it and how others are impacted by it. This is all part of the intricate balance for us students, and our lives since February 14. We are navigating our way through our grief, which includes guilt, and we are learning to use our platform. Where do the dots connect the guilt, pity, and opportunity? I make up rules and ask myself similar questions daily. My latest question: "Is journalism just an excuse to get my name in a book?" But then I remember I have loved journalism since before the shooting, and that will never change. Also, I agreed to take part in writing this book, and I have to put in the work. It's no easy job.

There are many lines and branches tying these ideas together, but they all lead us back to the same concept. We were offered these opportunities, and we accepted them.

The world is less complicated than we make it out to be. Our lives are painful. We have experienced loss—this cannot be undone. And we have experienced change, which cannot be forgotten. Instead of questioning, honor the lost, remember, and be grateful. We are here because life must go on, and the world keeps turning; living means going on and turning with the world. We can live and remember, but we can't live our lives stuck on February 14. The world didn't stop, and neither can we—not only for us, but for them.

EXTRAORDINARY ACTS

Culinary Arts Teacher Ashley Kurth Pulls Students Fleeing Freshman Building into Safety

by Jordyn Laudanno

Photo by Mallory Muller

On Valentine's Day, culinary arts teacher Ashley Kurth was cooking with her fourth-period class. They were preparing shrimp scampi and bang bang shrimp for their lab assignment. Kurth usually stood by her classroom door to ensure that her class's cooking would not set the fire alarm off by accident while they were deep frying.

"I just kicked my doorstop away, and I heard two pops and then the fire alarm went off. I leaned my head in to jokingly shout at the kids, 'Who set the fire alarm off?'" Kurth said.

But then Kurth saw a student running toward her, screaming

that there was a shooter in the school. She immediately assumed it was the live drill she had been prepared for.

"I started gathering everyone in my room, thinking it was the live action drill, and then the shots continued faster, which was something I was not used to."

She proceeded to walk to the front of her classroom to make sure its two doors were locked. But as she looked through her peripheral vision, she realized a whole group of students were running away from the Freshman Building.

"Some of the children running had debris and things on them, which was kinda the clue to me that this was not a drill.... Any students who were running toward the Freshman Building, I physically grabbed and pulled them into my classroom," Kurth said.

After about 90 seconds of madness, when the traffic outside her classroom ceased, Kurth decided to close her door. She attempted to calm all of the students in her room, which quickly increased from 29 to 65 students.

"One student was having a panic attack, and we assessed her to make sure she was okay because we knew we were secure and locked in the room, even though the gunfire was still going on," Kurth said.

Kurth hid with AP Environmental Science teacher Tammy Orilio and women's basketball coach Marilyn Rule. They decided to take out Kurth's laptop and record the names of the students they had in the room to make sure administrators knew the students' location.

"We tried to hear what was going on through the radio. We pulled up the clip from Channel Seven to see what was going on through an aerial view. I tried to get the students, instead of worrying about Snapchat, to check in on everyone they could to see where they were," Kurth said.

Kurth admits she had a lot of contemplation during the short amount of time the shooting started.

"I did not know if I should grab everyone and make them run, but listening to the proximity of the gunshots and our location, I knew there was no way I was letting anyone out," Kurth said. "The longer I stood at the door, I was getting very nervous. It was just standing there playing with my mind, like how long do you stand there until you have to close it?"

After they stayed in hiding for two hours, the SWAT team came to their rescue and escorted everybody out of the culinary room. Then MSD students and faculty were made fully aware of the tragedy that occurred.

Kurth, along with other teachers, went back to school for the first time the week before the students. "It was hard. I feel very comforted in my own classroom because the way that it is structured and the location, it is very safe. It's very difficult leaving my room and going to different areas. Driving up to the school, I do still get a little bit of anxiety," Kurth said.

The events of that day will remain with MSD for a long time, but Kurth continues to be impressed by the actions of her students as they heal from this tragedy.

"I am very saddened that it took something like this to make the students come together and be passionate, [but] I think how the students are reacting is amazing."

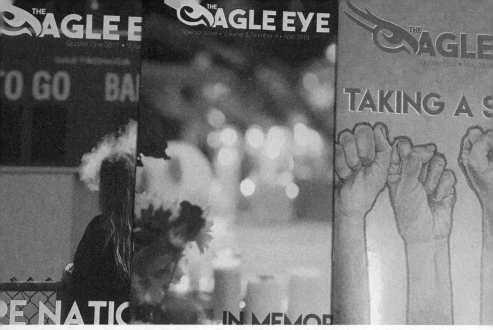

THE EVOLUTION OF THE *EAGLE EYE* WEBSITE

by Christy Ma

Before February 14, traffic on the *Eagle Eye* website was very low, and it was not always considered a valuable resource by students or the broader community. A large portion of the student population at Marjory Stoneman Douglas High School, the school the *Eagle Eye* reports on, did not know the website existed, let alone read every article that was published. After the tragedy that occurred on Valentine's Day, when national headlines about MSD reached hundreds of thousands of readers by the minute, only the *Eagle Eye* had the unique insider's perspective to bring depth and context to the personal accounts our students wanted to share.

As student journalists and survivors, we considered this our most important assignment ever.

Even before the first stories on the shooting were assigned, the newspaper staff unanimously agreed to never mention the shooter's name in any of our stories. We believed including his name would give him the attention he wanted, even if it would not be in a positive light. People who commit such heinous actions should not have the privilege of having their names uttered, much less promoted on a national scale. Instead, we focused on reporting the healing, activism, and extraordinary acts that emerged from that tragic day.

The *Eagle Eye* added two extra tabs on the website labeled "MSD Strong" and "Politics & Activism," with three subcategories underneath "MSD Strong" labeled "Extraordinary Acts," "Healing," and "Our Story." The addition of these categories was not just as simple as adding a few new tabs online, although that is what it may seem like on the surface. The new categorization method for our stories symbolized how the school was changed permanently after the shooting. To reflect that change, our website and newspaper will no longer only focus on news, features, sports, editorials, and arts and leisure. There will always be stories featured under "MSD Strong," student activists screaming for change, and a permanent transformation in the staff's writing.

The media has often overlooked the other 3,300 students who survived on February 14 while focusing solely on the March For Our Lives organizers, but the experiences of the other students that day are just as valuable as those shared by the more high-profile activists. The *Eagle Eye* strives to amplify the voices of all our survivors, and to highlight the unity within the community that arose from this tragedy. We have featured teachers who put their students' safety first and witnessed their classrooms destroyed by bullets, students who had to take on the challenge of emotional and even physical recoveries, and students and teachers who went on large media platforms to keep the talk about gun control alive—all to exemplify the resilience and passion MSD has to offer.

Another one of our goals since Valentine's Day was to be a source of information for students, whether on the election process, Congress's stance on gun reform legislation, or ways to get involved with organizations for other issues besides gun control. It is our job as journalists to report on important topics accurately to keep our community well informed.

Our decision to focus our coverage on the aftermath of the shooting rather than on the shooter was a means for us to move beyond the image of our school as just the site of another American school shooting. We wanted to be remembered for the activism that arose out of the tragedy, not for the perpetrator's actions. Months after the shooting, a video the shooter recorded of himself before Valentine's Day was released to the public. In it, he says that one of his motives for committing this terrible crime was for his name to be remembered by all. Unfortunately, some media outlets have fulfilled his wish by giving him the attention he so desperately sought. The editorial board strongly believes in refraining from contributing to his notoriety, which influenced our decision to focus on all other aspects of the school shooting, including student and faculty stories, recovery efforts, community outreach, and student activism. Through this, the *Eagle Eye* coverage has moved beyond the violence and its aftermath to chronicle the start of a revolution.

THE PARKLAND MARCH FOR OUR LIVES: TWO PERSPECTIVES

by Augustus Griffith Jr. and Sam Grizelj

HEALING IN MOTION, BY AUGUSTUS GRIFFITH JR.

The Parkland March For Our Lives was a surprisingly impactful event organized by highly influential teens. When we arrived at the opening ceremonies early, the atmosphere was defiant, without any doubts or turmoil. The force of our defiance in the face of tragedy was inescapable, and the dissatisfaction with our legislature was bottomless. Perhaps the most surprising thing was the passion of thousands of proud students, parents, and teachers, many of whom had traveled from as far as the West Coast just to take to the streets and stand firm for what they believe in. It was certainly energizing to see just how many people were joining our uphill battle.

The speakers reminisced about their loved ones and empowered the crowd by promising to push the movement forward in their names. They swore to march for those we'd lost, cautiously reminding us to never let our voices go silent, our stories untold. To never be dissuaded from starting a movement. It was with those final words that the march commenced and we took to the streets, demanding change. Not a single person in attendance would go unheard. We had all lost too much to give up or slow down.

The perfect blend of parents, teachers, and students took up signs, not arms, with at least seventeen reasons to demand action against the severe lack of leadership around the issue of a gun control. People who had entered the event complete strangers walked side by side, arm in arm, celebrating their similarities instead of arguing about their differences. The #NeverAgain movement was a large step forward, in both activism and healing. On March 24, survivors and supporters alike were one in fluid movement.

Photo by Josh Riemer

TAKING BACK OUR POWER: THE PARKLAND MARCH FOR OUR LIVES, BY SAM GRIZELJ

"We want change! We want change!" The chant flowed through the streets of Parkland, Florida, as citizens lifted their signs into the air, taking their chance to be heard. Their individual voices joined together and stayed strong through the entire march, becoming even more powerful as they marched through the streets of Parkland. They helped us persevere because they told us we weren't alone. People across the nation—and all over the world—joined our fight, too.

The people were demanding change and were willing to do whatever it took to make a difference in a peaceful manner. It did not matter how young or old they were, or who they were—what mattered was their support for the cause. As the citizens marched through our town, I could hear their passion and I could feel the fiery spirit that yearned for a revolution. These people demanded answers and demanded change within our nation. Camera in hand, I had the ability to reveal to the world what these people were fighting for.

While filming, I found out that people from all over the country had gathered in Parkland to march alongside the students from Marjory Stoneman Douglas High School. It amazed me how people from different states had come to Parkland to show their support. Each person had their own reason for protesting. As for me, I wanted to reveal the strength hidden within the Stoneman Douglas community. Stoneman Douglas students can overcome anything with their strong will and vigorous spirit. We are going to power through this tragedy in order to prove our determination to get something accomplished. Whether it would be to tear down and rewrite our faulty gun-control laws, improve school security, or attain better mental health care, we all wanted something to be done. Although I was at the march to advocate for change, I was also there to commemorate the lives that were lost in the tragic incident.

As we marched, strangers saw me wearing my #MSDStrong shirt and asked if I was from Stoneman Douglas. When I said yes, I noticed how their expressions quickly change from curiosity to amazement. The other students told me how impressed they were with the courage we displayed by returning to the school after what happened. They could not even imagine going back to school if it had happened to them and said we were heroes. I was so astonished at the response that I didn't know what to say. I never would have thought that others would consider us to be fearless.

I overheard other protesters saying that they had decided to march in Parkland because of how much effort was put into this event, and that we were heroes for banding together to revolt against the government. I began to feel more grateful for those who decided to march with us in Parkland—not only did they view our bold actions as something heroic, but I appreciated their time and effort in coming out to march with us and helping us when we needed it most.

As we continued to protest through the streets of Parkland, students spoke about wanting to end the need to live in constant fear. Teenagers shouldn't have to be concerned with whether we are going to survive to the next day. We should worry about what we are going to wear to prom, what we are going to do for graduation, or what college we are going to. Attempting to replace faulty laws should not be our responsibility, but it's a task that was put on our collective shoulders, a task none of us asked for. We are the generation that will decide who stays and who goes. And we will be instrumental in choosing the next generation of leaders.

The March For Our Lives was an event filled with passion and determination to finally set things right. It allowed us to speak our minds on issues that need to be resolved once and for all, and even though it is now over, the fight for our safety isn't. That battle will continue until we finally get gun control, universal background checks, better options for mental health regulation, and improvements in school security. This was one battle of many that we have to endure in this war. After all, this is a fight for our lives, and a search for justice.

EXTRAORDINARY ACTS

Ernie Rospierski, Social Studies Teacher, Shields Students from Shooter

by Einav Cohen

Photo by Suzanna Barna

On February 14, 2018, social studies teacher Ernie Rospierski was on the third floor of the Freshman Building in room 1249 when the fire alarm went off. His students began packing their things and evacuating the room. As Rospierski left the classroom and reached the stairwell, he immediately recognized the sound of gunshots from below.

All the students who had started to leave began running back up the stairs, and Rospierski waited at the end of the hallway, drawing as many kids as he could into classrooms to take cover.

He walked behind the students, yelling loudly for them to reach safety and get into a room.

By the time Rospierski got back to his classroom door, the shooter had gone up the stairs and reached the end of the hallway. Rospierski was unable to identify him because his face was covered by a gas mask.

"At the time I didn't realize it was an active shooter. I thought it was the Code Red drill that we had been worried about," Rospierski said. "So I was trying to make sure our kids were going to the safest place they could. I wasn't worried about me at the time."

But Rospierski finally came to terms with what was happening when one of his former students was shot behind him. With students from his class still in the hallway, Rospierski frantically grabbed as many of them as possible and put them into the alcove by his classroom door to hide them from the bullets.

The shooter then took aim at Rospierski, grazing him on the cheek and hip. After another four or five shots, there was suddenly silence. Rospierski peeked his head out of the alcove to get a look at the shooter and saw that he was fiddling with the weapon, most likely reloading.

Recognizing the chance that this small window of time offered, Rospierski told his kids to run toward the left stairwell and he followed behind them. He attempted to shield as many kids as possible with his body until they all reached the stairwell.

Then he put his foot against the stairwell door to stop the shooter from following the students to give them time to escape.

The shooter tried to pry the door open several times, but

Rospierski's strength and determination to protect his students forced the shooter to give up. Because of Rospierski's bravery, no more students were injured.

"[The shooter] decided to push against the door and try and get through, but he couldn't get through because my foot was there," Rospierski said. "After that, I waited 'one thousand one, one thousand two, one thousand three' until he stopped trying to get through the door, and then I ran down the stairs, to find my own form of a hiding hole."

The students who ran down the west stairwell were led outside by a SWAT team when they reached the ground floor. Three of Rospierski's students were killed and another was injured on that tragic day. Even though he is processing the events well, he admits that he will never feel the same again.

"I don't think of myself as anything besides just a normal person doing what they could to help others. That's what I think anyone would do in that situation," Rospierski said. "It's not just my job; I expect any of my peers, people that I like, people who are my friends, to react the same way. And it's not about being a hero, it's about doing what's right. . . . It's not listed in the job requirements, it's something we just do."

Photo by Kevin Trejos

HEALING THROUGH JOURNALISM

by Suzanna Barna

It's hard to define what normal is after the most abnormal and tragic senior year, but I kept hearing that chilling phrase: "new normal." I found that as the days passed and distance grew between the present and the shooting, life grew routine once again, classes started, and the pressures of school piled onto the quest for personal health. Yet it was merely a month ago that I struggled to speak with my family about anything, as I relied heavily on my friends and peers who had endured the same experience as me.

   Part of my process of grieving and recovery included my role as a student journalist for the *Eagle Eye*. After being locked in our camera closet in the newspaper classroom during the shooting, it was a relief to go back to school and feel safe and accepted in that same room. By keeping our workload intense and significant, I felt needed, and that gave me a lot of hope and relief.

Newspaper aided me in establishing that infamous new normal people kept saying was going to arrive. The class and work assignments it provided, even before school had begun again, helped give me structure and work to invest myself in rather than sobbing or thinking about the past. I focused my energy on something constructive instead of wallowing in my own pain and avoided spiraling into a never-ending realm of thoughts and prayers.

By writing about and photographing the events since the shooting, I have found solace and closure. Two of my major articles for Newspaper were writing the memorial profile about Gina Montalto, a freshman who died on February 14, and covering the March For Our Lives in Parkland on March 24.

When I discovered that we as a staff would create a memorial issue for the seventeen victims of the shooting, I felt honored yet worried about writing about one of the victims who lost their life. The task seemed daunting, since any mistake would absolutely be noticed and the subject was as serious as can be. But the assignment actually helped me become in tune with the emotions I had tried to suppress, as I was able to learn all about Gina and share the impact she had on the world and on the people who loved her. I felt good to be able to honor her. And I hoped by reporting on Gina in an honest and thorough way that would forever stay with whoever read the profile, I could bring some peace to her family and friends. The Montalto family were more private than some other victims' families. In fact, it was difficult to get in touch with Gina's parents, but I was fortunate to find a friend of Gina's who helped me reach them. This led to my first interview with them, which was their first interview with anyone. Writing about Gina helped me to cope with the tragedy and the emotions I had and mourn while respecting her legacy.

Journalism requires impartiality and objectivity, which sounds contradictory with the emotions and sensitivities involved in covering the events following the shooting. Although remaining impartial and unbiased wasn't essential while writing Gina's memorial article, it was essential for writing my Parkland March For Our Lives article. When I covered this event, I interviewed people about what the march meant to them following the loss in our community. Many spoke about how uplifting the day was. I also used quotes from speeches to compose my article and kept it fact-based as opposed to politicized or biased. By writing an article that focused on the experiences of others and the speeches given that day, I could remain objective in my style and diction and felt I produced a well-focused and informative piece of journalism about an important event for the greater Parkland community.

I also took many photos during this period of recovery. Photography allowed me to capture the moments around me and document every aspect on the scene without emotionally draining myself too much. I can now look back at the photos and reflect on the recent past and the feelings that went along with it. It's hard to describe how a photograph encloses everything in that one point in time: the emotions, the actions, the ambience, all in a single click of a button and forever recorded.

Through all of these endeavors in Newspaper, from going

back to school, writing articles, and photographing the world, I have healthfully adapted to life after the tragedy of Valentine's Day. Journalism allowed me to be useful in the days following the shooting and let me do something constructive for my broken community.

WHAT IT'S LIKE TO WORK WITH MASS MEDIA

by Zakari Kostzer

Working with the media is in some ways like a football game or a soccer match. The matches are stressful and competitive, yet when someone gets hurt, most of the players from both teams will go to help the injured player. But there are always one or two players who don't. This is also true about working with media. The ability to connect with such a great community of journalists would not have happened if it were not for my position in making the *#MSDStrong* documentary. But there are some news teams that have been less than helpful.

Following the tragic event at our school, Mr. Eric Garner—

who I usually call Garner—texted a few students from his higher-level classes, saying that he would like to make a documentary, and he would like us to do it. A few days after returning to school, the other students, Garner, and I sat down to discuss what we wanted to do. As a producer, I handled most of the communication with local affiliates and national news organizations and developed the story line.

After the release of the *#MSDStrong* documentary, Garner and I started to receive emails, text messages, and DMs from different media outlets, asking to interview us about the process and concept of the documentary. Garner, another producer, and I ran around Coral Springs and Parkland for a couple of days to speak to them. We were also contacted by other media outlets who wanted to spread the message of our documentary. As time passed, the coverage got less and less, until the March For Our Lives in Parkland.

Beep! Beep! Beep! That loud, obnoxious sound no one wants to wake up to came way too early on March 24. As I sluggishly got ready, I lost myself in thought, not knowing what the day had in store for me. I had to have my dad drop me off at the media staging area early in the morning to make sure that two other students and I were set with our press credentials for the event. One of my good friends was able to put me in contact with Casey Sherman, one of the event's organizers, to help us gain our credentials. Once we got there, we were welcomed with open arms.

Much like a soccer game when a player gets injured, almost everyone wanted to help us. All the local affiliates were so nice and helpful. Standing next to professionals and learning from them was such an amazing experience. They were curious about what we were doing and how we were doing. Rather than being concerned with the story, they were concerned with us, journalist to journalist. But there were a couple of journalists who sat in the back and disrespected us and only cared about their story.

Covering the Parkland march, I truly learned what Garner meant when he told us, "If you go into the industry, it's going to be tough sometimes, but you better get the shot the production team needs because your job depends on it." When the student leaders and the rest of the student body approached the starting line, we raced up to the front to get the perfect shot when, from behind me, I could hear and feel the other journalists jockeying for the best positions. Although some news teams tried to push us out of the way, focused solely on their own need to report, I could hear others defending us, saying that we were MSD students and needed to be given access to the event that we had helped to create. It gave me more confidence in the media to see that not everybody was a coldhearted reporter. And I have since been able to meet amazing people in the field who have impressed me and reinforced my interest in broadcasting in the future.

USING WORK ON THE DOCUMENTARY AS AN ESCAPE

by Chris Cahill

Working has always been my way of dealing with problems. As long as I can keep some momentum, either with schoolwork or videos, I can usually charge through any trouble I face. When Mr. Garner, my Television Production teacher, pitched the documentary to me, I was actually quite relieved. In those first two weeks before we returned to school, I had tried to start several projects to keep myself occupied, anything to keep my mind from mulling over what had happened. But no matter what I did, I couldn't stay on task. When I tried to do research on mass shootings, I would start putting myself in the victims' place. If I tried looking into the lives of the victims to find a way to honor them, I would be overcome by tears. Worst of all, if I wasn't completely occupied for even a single minute, I began playing out even more tragic situations than what had happened, because for some god-awful reason, as everyone else was thinking, "How could such a terrible thing happen?" I was thinking about all the ways it could have been worse.

Working on the documentary gave me an escape from the fallout of the shooting, but it was much more than that: it was structured and official. As a producer, I was trusted to make sure it would get done. I was able to be with my second family the entire time I was at school, and it kept me too busy for my mind to wander. In hindsight, I was clearly suppressing emotions in the first month after the shooting; pushing myself to work on the documentary drew those emotions out and allowed me to deal with them.

I started out doing well, but I very quickly took on too much and became overwhelmed. I ultimately had to step down from the project almost entirely. This failure forced me to reevaluate myself and conclude that I wasn't okay. I had been surrounded by people who had much more intense experiences than I did that day; in contrast, I felt like I was barely affected. I felt that I had a responsibility to carry on while others couldn't *because* they couldn't, and the fact that I wasn't capable of moving forward meant that I was somehow failing them.

My fourth-period class was in the next building over from where the shooting took place. Upon hearing the fire drill, we exited the south side of the 700 building and headed for the staircase on the northeast side of the building. Students screaming and running up the stairs turned us away from that direction. We all started walking in the opposite direction, away from the Freshman Building, but were deterred once again, this time by an administrator coming up the stairs near the office and yelling at us to return to our classrooms.

My teacher guided us back to her room. As she fumbled with the keys, we heard a string of gunshots from around the corner. She got the door open, and we disappeared into the room. At this point I was thinking the shots were either blanks or someone banging on the old lockers. I didn't even consider the possibility of it being real, but I still texted my parents to let them know I was okay. For the next two hours, all we heard were sirens and helicopters. I think it finally hit me as we were all huddled around a cell phone, watching a livestream of our own school on the news. Every ten minutes or so I'd get a text from my mother checking if I was *still* okay. Our room was finally cleared at about 4:30, guided to safety by a wall of police officers. From the door of our classroom to the perimeter fence, we had a police officer within five feet of us at all times. I've never seen so many police officers; some of them were in normal clothes and just had a tactical vest on. The sight of so many police officers was both a relief and absolutely terrifying.

I knew from texting my dad that he was stuck about a mile away at the next intersection, so I started walking toward him. I passed by a lot of parents, tears streaming down their faces, sprinting toward the school. As I approached the intersection, I began to see more people. Journalists were pulling kids off the sidewalk, frantic to find an angle no other outlet had gotten.

It was disgusting. That day I completely swore off ever covering a tragedy if I became a journalist.

The first twenty-four hours seemed like they'd never end. The entire world felt like it was moving faster than usual and I couldn't keep up, like I was caught in quicksand in the middle of a hurricane. Therapy, memorials, a vigil—how was this all happening so fast? It almost seemed as if everyone was trying to put this behind them as quickly as possible. I spent a lot of time in the park next to my house just wandering around, trying to clear my head; I found a basketball by a court and started bouncing it. Everything was fine, and then the ball hit the ground just the right way and I heard the string of gunshots again and went to the ground. *What? No, I'm fine, I didn't even think the gunshots were real when I heard them. There was never a moment during that lockdown when I thought I was going to die. What reason do I have not to be okay?*

For the next week and a half, I quietly watched all the rallies and political activism from my phone. I knew I should follow my peers' lead and get involved, but I just couldn't bring myself to get out and fight back, or even cover the story. I only really left the house to visit the memorial at our school and to attend funerals. I felt completely powerless. *I should be out there, doing whatever I can. I have no reason to be this sluggish,* I kept thinking.

When we returned to the school to retrieve our belongings and Mr. Garner first told me about the documentary, I couldn't wait to get started. Finally, I would have something to work on. I'd force myself to do it if I had to. The only reason I was even able to get up on our first day back in school was the anticipation of getting to work on something important. We had a meeting after school to brainstorm how we were going to do this. None of us had ever done anything on this scale, and we obviously had to be careful since it was such a sensitive subject. The community was already sick of the media, so as the only group that had permission to film on campus, we had to be extremely respectful. Fortunately, we had the help of alumni and several other high schools across the country. Mr. Garner had already explained how he wanted to break the documentary into parts. Our portion of the documentary was simple: the students' return to the school.

Returning to school was interesting. We weren't doing anything academic in any of my classes, so I'd ask permission to go to TV Production, and it was usually granted. Being able to talk and work with my TV family all day was amazing. Just being with them, working and joking, was therapeutic. We were surprisingly efficient and finished everything except for editing. I had volunteered to take care of that on my own time. However, I soon realized I was not able to keep up the same efficiency at home. I'd be perfectly fine at school, but the moment I got home, I crashed, getting practically nothing done for hours. *I'm okay. Am I not okay? What is going on? Why can't I just focus?*

With only four days left to finish our segment, I still couldn't get any editing done. Then it was three days, then two, then . . . I got a call from a friend of mine checking in to make sure I was still planning on working that weekend. I was almost relieved when I was reminded that I had to work as a climbing instructor at a camp halfway across the state and wouldn't be in school on the Friday that the film was due. I walked in Thursday morning and told the team that I wouldn't be in school on Friday and someone else would have to finish editing, and they were more understanding about me dropping a ton of work on them with a day to do it than I probably would have been.

Throughout that weekend, I really beat myself up over dropping the ball on the documentary. It was selfish of me to not just admit that I couldn't do it and ask for help. If I had said something on Monday or Tuesday, I'm sure they would have understood. More importantly, what the hell happened with me? I've never completely broken down like that before. I finally admitted that maybe I wasn't as okay as I thought, and that weekend my healing process actually began. While I ultimately may have not been essential in the finished product of the documentary, it was an essential part of my healing process, and I am very glad that I had the opportunity to work on it.

PART THREE

What Comes Next

STARTING A GRASSROOTS MOVEMENT
A Quick Guide

by Delaney Tarr

1. **Find your cause.** While it sounds easy to just find a cause, there's a lot more to it. For us it was easy: We were thrown into the world of gun control because of a tragedy we experienced. But that's not always the case for activists. Many pick a cause purely because it matters to them, be it through ideologies or experience. That—picking a cause that matters—is the key to a grassroots movement. It's easy to tell when someone isn't passionate about their cause, so it's important to not just pick one randomly. Think about it. What matters to you?

What can you dedicate yourself to fully? Once you find what you care about the most, anything is possible.

2. **Control your message.** In the world of social media, "fake news," and constant agenda pushing, it's easy to be manipulated. Even the kindest people have some sort of personal agenda or point of view, and that can influence how your words are received. However, the beauty of a grassroots movement is that it is so grounded. The strongest tool a grassroots activist can use is social media. There is no third-party manipulation or misinterpretation, no filter between the speaker and the audience. It is purely your words and message being said to your intended audience. That way, you can communicate clearly and concisely, with as little room for confusion as possible.

3. **Stay true to your roots.** As your movement grows, things will get significantly more complicated. There will inevitably be some levels of bureaucracy added, some professionals hired. A sign of success is the need for this extra help. But it is absolutely vital to not lose what makes your movement a "grassroots" one. Often, organizations will become so large and official that they lose the core of their movement and simply become another multimillion-dollar corporation. To stay true to your roots, you must keep the group close-knit. Try to hold on to those core people, the ones who have been along for the whole journey. Stay close to the community, valuing them over the temptation of money and fame. But most important, keep the connection to your audience. A movement is nothing

if people don't feel connected to it, if people don't care. The more distance that is added with hierarchy and celebrity, the less people may feel personally touched by the cause.

4. **Mobilize, mobilize, mobilize.** The term "mass mobilization" is thrown around a lot by activists. While it seems a bit vague, it's an essential idea. The point of a movement is to make the public active. Keeping not only an engaged audience but an involved audience is the only way to make progress on both a national and global scale. A small group of close-knit people can only make so much change. It falls onto the activism of people in their own communities to make change everywhere.

5. **Let others be leaders.** It's easy to get caught up in being the face of a national movement. The mix of responsibility and power that comes with it is stressful but addictive. Yet it's not something to take on alone. No matter how strong your voice is, it cannot speak for all. Other people with their own stories, their own experiences, can only serve to broaden the horizons of your movement. Empowering other leaders, be they adults, teens, or even children, can ensure the success of the movement on every level. It also encourages leadership in many different areas that can work well into the future, making the world a better place.

EXTRAORDINARY ACTS

Sgt. Jeff Heinrich, Off-Duty Officer, Saves Student and Secures Building

by Nikhita Nookala

Photo by Marilyn Rule

Sgt. Jeff Heinrich of the Coral Springs Police Department is a police officer with a unique connection to Marjory Stoneman Douglas High School. His wife, Marilyn Rule, is a world history teacher and the assistant athletic director, and his son is a student at the high school. In his spare time during the day, Heinrich likes to help the staff keep up the grounds of the athletic fields. On February 14, Heinrich was doing just that. He was off-duty, wearing shorts and a T-shirt, and watering the infield of the baseball diamond when he first heard a round of three or four shots. Initially, he was in disbelief.

"I honestly thought they were fireworks," Heinrich said at the February 15 press conference. "I thought the kids were screwing around; I thought maybe someone set off some fireworks, and the school set off the fire alarm."

Upon approaching the 1200 building, however, Heinrich quickly discovered that the noise was, in fact, gunshots, and soon after he encountered an injured student. The student, now known to be freshman Kyle Laman, had been shot in the leg. Despite his injury, Laman provided Heinrich with a detailed description of the shooter and where he encountered him. Heinrich tended to Laman's injuries with first-aid supplies found in the clubhouse near the baseball field, and then turned him over to fire department paramedics.

Heinrich, now fully focused on upholding his law enforcement duties, met with Capt. Bradley McKeone, who gave him an extra bulletproof vest and a weapon for him to protect himself. Heinrich choked up at the press conference as he described the next part of his experience: calling his wife and son. He was able to reach his family and was relieved to find that they had reunited by pure chance, safe and waiting along with two other teachers and 63 students.

Heinrich then returned to the 1200 building, and while deputies were inside the school clearing the hallways, Heinrich, Captain McKeone, and an unnamed Broward Sheriff Office deputy maintained the perimeter of the building. Once it was determined that the shooter had left campus, Heinrich, along with the BSO officers, began to clear the other buildings in the school, evacuating students and teachers with the assistance of the SWAT team and the K9 unit. Heinrich was reunited with his family much later that evening in their Coral Springs home.

Heinrich's heroic actions are heralded by police and local press, as well as the MSD community. The officer later paid a visit to Laman in the hospital and keeps in touch with his parents. While the investigation continues, Heinrich is using social media to try to fulfill Laman's three biggest wishes: meeting Donald Trump, meeting Ellen DeGeneres, and getting a German shepherd service dog.

BECOMING AN ACTIVIST IN YOUR SCHOOL

by Suzanna Barna

The role of an activist isn't what you see on TV or on social media. Although the media works beautifully for advocacy and helps spread messages widely, true activism starts from within, built up from a motivation and a passion for civic engagement and social change. An activist knows that significant changes can begin in the smallest ways and through simple actions.

A great place to start for anyone who wants to get involved in a cause is in school. Yes, it may seem surprising, but joining clubs and organizations at school can help in a multitude of ways.

Let's say a student has recently discovered the danger of oil spills after watching a documentary, and that student now wants to send aid to the facilities that care for the animal victims of a spill. This person would want to find an organization devoted to environmental protection and conservation. Some clubs relating to the environment and science that can be found on a high school campus include the Science National Honor Society, the Science Club, and Save What's Left. Through these clubs, students can lead a drive to gather supplies to send to the rescue facilities, make friends with others who share an interest in the cause, and learn more about the nature of oil spills and oceanic ecosystems to spark future activism.

I've been heavily involved in the National Honor Society and Key Club at MSD and have worked with the elderly at a local senior citizen community, Aston Gardens. As I have discovered, extracurricular activities can provide students with valuable opportunities for leadership roles. By growing through officer and committee positions, I have learned to feel more comfortable with public speaking, a lifelong fear of mine that is shared by many people. Leadership forces direct communication with peers, administration and teachers, and large crowds. I've found that speaking in front of my clubs has helped me find the courage I needed to share my voice and my ideas.

After the shooting, this ability played a vital role as the media swarmed the Parkland community. When interview offers came about, I was hesitant to take any—nervous about what to say and whether I was emotionally ready. At the time I decided to do my first interview, I felt nervous leading up to the filming, but once it all began, the words flowed naturally. I knew I had to speak alongside my peers, and I had plenty to say, as it was less than a week after the shooting and the frustrations and grief were fresh wounds. My ability to improvise responses to questions and speak in a coherent and respectful way helped me convey my desired message to the people who watched my interviews.

Many extracurricular activities have events and service projects that relate to their club's mission. Participation in the community is essential to activism, as it builds character and connections at a local level, as well as time management and organizational skills. My service with the elderly includes a variety of weekly events and special holiday events throughout the year. In addition to my AP classes and a part-time job, I've been able to commit time to the aging generations I've always cared deeply about by utilizing time-management skills and organizational and interpersonal skills to create my service project. Planning and managing projects will not only help you become an activist and leader, but will also help you conduct yourself professionally and respectfully in work and life.

Due to our age, students often are barred from pursuing their ideas, limiting the extent of activism and advocacy they may provide for a cause. That's why clubs, where students serve the community and gain leadership in school, can be an important place to begin ideas and initiatives. Students starting a national movement like March For Our Lives is not commonplace, but any student can get involved in their own community and find a way to make the lives around them better.

Clubs and organizations can also be a great place to form friendships with people who share similar values. This unity in a club creates a safe space for ideas and knowledge to flourish.

Student clubs have members with varying degrees of

knowledge and experience. If students know a lot about a cause they are passionate about, a club is a great place to put their knowledge to good use to create something personally meaningful or to benefit the school or the community. Alternatively, if you care about something and don't know exactly how to help, a club can assist you in that research. So as you learn and grow on your own, your peers can complement your ideas with new perspectives and solutions.

But what if your cause does not have a club or organization? Well, if there isn't a club, make one. It is not as difficult as it might seem. Find a teacher or school administrator and ask them what steps you should take to establish a new club. Get a group of friends who can help you organize and plan meetings and events. Make your cause heard in your school and in the community, and enjoy your time working for a cause you love with people who share your passion.

Above all else, value your days in school before it is too late. Knowledge is power, and when combined with work ethic and motivation, you can accomplish anything you strive to achieve. The knowledge and skills gained from your experience in school clubs will give you an advantage as you launch into a career, while enabling your activist activities to flourish, helping to make the world a better place sooner and effectively.

A GUIDE TO REACHING OUT
AND SPEAKING TO POLITICIANS

by Lewis Mizen

1. **Use your resources.** The first step in talking to politicians is
    reaching out to them, whether through social media, email,
    phone calls, friends, families, or even people you know. If you
    have an issue that you care about, identify the people who
    can make a difference in politics and find a way to connect
    with them. Establishing contact is the first step, and once you
    do that you can begin a discussion that can bring about the
    change you are trying to enact.

2. **Know who you are meeting.** Knowing which politician you

are reaching out to is a lot more than simply knowing their name. To know the kind of person they are and what their beliefs are can go a long way toward making a lasting impression and getting them over to your side. The people you will be meeting are public figures, so you can know a lot more about them than they do about you when making contact. Use that to your advantage.

3. **Be respectful.** This should go without saying. Whether or not you agree with their political beliefs or personal ideologies, it is important to be respectful. In order to have meaningful dialogue and actually make some progress in achieving your goal, it's important to treat people with respect. Remember that they are in positions of power, and you should respect them as such.

4. **Don't be overly awed.** Building off of the previous point, while it's important to be respectful, you should remember that these are people, too, and they have flaws just like you. In theory, you are both just citizens of your community trying to do what you each think is best, and that mentality can help you find middle ground and make compromises that can lead to real, substantive change. They are going to make mistakes, too, and while those mistakes should be pointed out to them, remember not to hold them against them. These are people with important jobs, but they are still people.

5. **Follow up.** After meeting with them or speaking to them on the phone, it is always good to follow up with an email. Not

only will it help them to remember you and the issue you were discussing, but it will also push the issue higher up their list of priorities. Remember, these politicians are your representatives, and they are supposed to represent your interests.

CONTROLLING THE INTERVIEW

How to Avoid Saying Something You Don't Believe

by Nikhita Nookala

Some journalists walk into an interview with a certain expectation. They might have a specific lens in mind when they pick someone to interview, and they expect that person to say something that supports that view. To ensure this, some journalists slant their questions to subtly lead the interviewee to answer in a way that is misleading or that does not represent his or her true feelings toward the subject.

Here are some tips to help you avoid interview pitfalls.

1. **Take a second to truly understand the question before an-**

swering. Being interviewed can be a high-stress situation, especially if it is on live television or radio. But there is nothing wrong with pausing to decide how to answer. Answering hastily can result in your saying something that can be misconstrued, especially if the question is one that addresses something personal to you or a topic that you have very strong feelings about.

2. **Avoid using "absolute" words.** "Always," "every time," "without fail"—those words would usually be the telltale sign of a wrong answer on a multiple-choice exam. Words that don't allow for exceptions. Using absolute terms when you are not completely positive that an exception has never occurred in a certain situation is a surefire way to get criticism from opposition. Instead, substitute "generally," "most times," and "rarely" to allow for mistakes in your research.

3. **Don't cite a specific case unless you know the context and history behind it.** Citing specific examples often prompts an interviewer to ask you to explain why you chose to bring it up, and sounding uninformed in those thirty seconds can cause the viewer or listener to discredit your entire opinion.

4. **Be especially wary of sentences starting with "So what you're saying is . . ."** This is where sound bites are born. If what the interviewer says doesn't encapsulate your message in a way that portrays you positively, then disagree and restate. This is not the time to be polite. Being shy can result in a viral clip that exploits this seemingly small misstep and overshadows

the rest of your interview. Your overall message can be forgotten in minutes by giving the wrong answer in this moment.

5. **Don't name names unless absolutely necessary.** When it comes to politics, being public about your disdain for a certain person can be a bridge burner. You might destroy future relationships or alliances by saying the wrong thing about the wrong person on the airwaves. Remember that interviews last forever. In this era of extreme partisanship, it's important to reach across the aisle whenever possible. If you want someone to work with you on a certain issue, insulting them is usually not a great step.

6. **Remember why you're there.** The reason you participate in an interview, especially regarding grassroots activism, is because you want to use the media's platform to promote your message. Never agree to an interview that you know will make you look bad. Researching the company or network conducting the interview is absolutely necessary. Are they sympathetic to your cause? And if not, do they respectfully allow opposing viewpoints to share their views? Or do they create deliberately misleading sound bites through selective editing, which can really affect the way you are viewed by people? If your platform isn't big enough to compete with that of traditional media, it can be impossible to combat criticism resulting from a maliciously edited piece.

7. **If you sense the interview is going in a direction you didn't expect or that you're not prepared for, try to redirect it to the**

message. This is something politicians do often, and it is a useful tool for anyone who has an agenda that they want to project. If a question is obviously attempting to push the conversation into controversial territory, push back with "I'm just here to talk about . . ." and reassert your issue. Especially as a student and a private citizen, you are not obligated to answer questions that make you uncomfortable or that paint you in a negative light.

Unlike public officials, you were not elected to do this; you chose to do this. It is imperative to remember that you are in control of your own media exposure. No one can make you say anything you don't want to say.

LEVERAGING SOCIAL MEDIA

by David Hogg

We were born into the first generation to experience both active-shooter drills *and* Twitter, and it was on the awful day—February 14, 2018—when absolute hell descended on our school that both of these facts of our lives intersected.

Because we had experienced so many drills—and had been promised a drill that would have people shooting blanks so that we might know what real gunshots sounded like—many of us at first didn't know if what was happening was real or not. Once we fully realized the horror of what had happened, we knew we could not remain quiet about it. To echo the old ACT UP slogan:

Silence = Death. And if we had said nothing, had just gone away and quietly descended into our shock and grief, then the shootings at our school would have gone away, too. Some of the most heinous mass murders in American history were in the news for just a number of days, and then fairly quickly they left public consciousness. And this pattern is what allows policy makers to get away with doing absolutely nothing in the face of horrible bloodshed. Their motives for inaction are not complicated—some have an absolutist idea of the Second Amendment and believe in unfettered access to as many privately owned weapons of war as you want. Some live in complete fear of the most powerful lobby in Washington and the state capitals—the National Rifle Association (NRA). And many fall into both categories.

My fellow students and I had no idea that when we chose to lift our voices we would be taking on the most influential, entrenched forces in America. We just knew intuitively that we could not remain silent. And that meant in addition to speaking to as many old-school journalists as would listen to us, we would utilize the social media tools with which my generation is fluent. For many of us, Twitter is virtually a second language that we grew up speaking. And yet these tools are so new that their effects are still being explored and measured. Could these tools level the playing field and enable a bunch of high school kids to take on a powerful lobby that had gone unchallenged for a generation? The same lobby that had shamelessly prevented *any* change to gun laws and background check laws, even after twenty firstgraders were murdered at Sandy Hook Elementary?

Could Twitter be the rock that David needs to take down Goliath?

These powerful forces have been around since long before we were born; these groups and allies have faced opposition before and outlasted it. And they count on people like us—the Columbine generation—to exhaust ourselves and go away, too.

NRA, if you're reading this: That is not going to happen.

I happen to be a space nerd, and by funny coincidence, a bunch of my schoolmates are space nerds, too. In fact, geeking out over our mutual love of SpaceX is how I first became friends with Emma González. Everyone told Elon Musk that launching and landing a reusable rocket was impossible. But everything hard was once considered impossible. Musk and his team ignored the conventional wisdom about what was possible and kept experimenting, kept innovating, and kept failing—until they succeeded. The sight of those two rockets simultaneously returning to earth and docking without so much as a scratch was a wonderful rebuke to the naysayers! It showed the power of persistence, ignoring the people who say something can't be done, and making the impossible possible.

And: Don't be afraid to fail. All learning comes from failure.

That is how you change the world.

We take inspiration from that spirit. I am *not* comparing our movement to SpaceX, but we have tried our best to model ourselves after them—setting our sights on a lofty goal that has not been achieved before, ignoring the powers that be, and not genuflecting to the way things have always been done. Of course, operating like that put us on a collision course with the NRA and lots of their supporters. And those guys don't mess around. They are used to winning, and they quickly proved that they weren't afraid to go after kids who were still mourning seventeen of their friends. Their incoming president, Oliver North, called us "civil terrorists" for having the gall to use our First Amendment rights to advocate for reasonable public safety measures to try to prevent yet another Parkland massacre from happening.

Of course, since becoming radicalized under CEO Wayne LaPierre, who joined the group in 1991, the NRA has assumed a never-give-an-inch policy. So essentially there is no talking to them, as there is simply no basis for reasonable conversation. In fact, the group is so unreasonable that in 1995, shortly after the bombing of the Murrah Federal Building in Oklahoma City, which was destroyed by a white supremacist with a massive fertilizer bomb, some lawmakers in Washington proposed adding taggants—tiny tracer pellets—to fertilizer, so that if it was used in future bombings law enforcement would be able to trace the fertilizer to see where it originated. The NRA opposed this policy, which is pretty mysterious, given that the NRA historically has had nothing to do with fertilizer. That same year, for good measure, LaPierre called federal ATF agents "jack-booted thugs" who wore "Nazi bucket helmets and black storm trooper uniforms to attack law-abiding citizens." Former President George H. W. Bush, a Republican, was so outraged by LaPierre's comments that to his great credit he immediately quit the NRA in disgust. That was in 1995, and if anything, the NRA has only gotten more paranoid and more extreme in the years since then.

And they have especially honed their defensive strategies since the school shooting era began in earnest with the horrifying massacre at Columbine High School in Littleton, Colorado, in April 1999.

So if there is no talking to them, then you have no choice but to defeat them. But how does a group of high school kids take on the lobby that has had Washington in a stranglehold for almost thirty years?

With humor and compassion and unity, as it turns out. And when they have all the money and all the power, you've got to be quicker, smarter, funnier, and more adept at the technologies that are native to our generation. For me and my sister, all of our wonderful friends at Marjory Stoneman Douglas High School, and all of the extraordinary young people we have met since the day our lives changed forever, that means making our case with Twitter and the other social media platforms available to us. I have had a sense of the connecting power of these platforms since I wandered onto Instagram in fifth grade and immediately started talking to somebody in Istanbul. These platforms are the great levelers and enable us to take on powerful people on a more or less equal footing. And these platforms are the greatest organizing tools ever invented, enabling us to reach people out in the world who are like-minded but who might have felt powerless and unable to make a difference on their own. When you realize that you are one of millions, then you begin to feel not so alone and not so powerless.

Just ask Leslie Gibson, a guy who was running for the Maine House of Representatives, who thought it was a good idea to attack Emma just three weeks after the murders at our school, calling her a "skinhead lesbian." I went on Twitter and put out a call for someone more qualified than that guy to run against him, and Gibson ended up dropping out of the race!

Or just ask Laura Ingraham, who thought it was a good idea to attack me on Twitter for being rejected from several colleges, and then saying that I whined about it. You can say many bad things about me and be accurate, but I am not a whiner. You might correctly call me petty, for instance, because when Ingraham attacked me, I posted a list of her advertisers, and the Twitter masses rose up in a glorious display of direct democracy and made their voices heard. In short order, Ingraham had a couple dozen fewer advertisers.

My generation wants to tackle this problem and change the world. And when I posted the social media accounts of all of her advertisers, that was a specific mission that everyone on our side understood immediately. It had nothing to do with curbing anyone's free speech. It had to do with the real-world consequences of that speech. Laura had used her platform to bully people for years without blowback. This time was different.

When people angrily attack you, especially when you have the courage of your convictions, we found that it is important not to respond with more anger. When that happens, humor is extremely important, as it signals that you do not take them or their "arguments" seriously. Obviously what they are saying is horrible, but if you point that out by laughing at them, you effectively prove your point and thoroughly confuse your attacker—because angry and paranoid people do not know what to do with humor. Comedy is the absolute best tactic in this kind of meme warfare. If you were angry back at them, it would be taking them seriously, and then the world would take them seriously, too. And you'd be making their platform even bigger.

Conversely, when they attack *you,* they make *your* platform bigger. And when they are powerful and have significant public platforms, and you are a high school student who is just trying to make the world a better place, then their attacks actually serve to bring you to public consciousness. When Emma was attacked and responded with sanity and grace, she went from not even having a Twitter account to having more followers than the NRA in under a week. When I was attacked, I went from having a normal high school kid's Twitter account to having more than 800,000 followers. For that, paradoxically, we owe the National Rifle Association and all of their pretty crazy online foot soldiers a big thank-you.

And let me add a word of compassion to the people online who have said some shockingly hateful things to me and my friends: That hate didn't occur spontaneously on the day we decided to speak out in favor of sanity in our gun policies. That hate comes from a place of deep unhappiness, and even trauma. Chances are, they would never say those things to you in person. Hatred is just like violence—it is something that we spread to each other like a disease. Hate loves company. And hate always goes in search of somebody to blame. That is the downside of social media— groups can organize like never before for positive change, but mobs can also form to do bad things. In any case, a human response to someone who shows you hatred can disarm the hate, and might even lead to actual understanding.

We don't have to agree on everything, and we may agree on nothing. But we can understand each other and get past our mutual caricatures. As we grow and learn and transform gun policy in America, we hope to also use the social media platforms to extend that kind of compassion to people who think we are wrong.

In the meantime, the young people will be changing the world.

EXTRAORDINARY ACTS

Charlie Rothkopf and Victoria Proietto Save Fellow Student During Shooting

by Abby Dowd

In times of tragedy, stories of heroism arise. During the horrifying act that took place on Valentine's Day 2018 at Marjory Stoneman Douglas High School, juniors Charlie Rothkopf and Victoria Proietto took the initiative to help sophomore Ashley Baez, who was suffering from a bullet wound.

As students of math teacher Nancy Lazar's fourth-period class, Rothkopf and Proietto were located in the Freshman Building at the time of the shooting. The class had not yet made their way out of the building to evacuate for what they believed was a fire drill when they heard gunshots. They returned to Lazar's classroom, along with fellow student Baez, who had been shot in the leg and fled to Lazar's room for help.

"My fourth period is Guitar, and we aren't allowed to use the bathroom in that hallway, so our options are to go to the Freshman Building or 700 Building," Baez said. "And I decided to go to the Freshman Building."

Baez happened to be using the bathroom located across the hallway from Lazar's classroom. Once she was injured, she fled to the nearest classroom to search for help. Rothkopf came to her aid by wrapping a yoga shirt from a fellow classmate tightly around her leg. He held the fabric there until the SWAT team came to rescue them.

"Everyone was freaking out, and I felt like I had to step up," Rothkopf said. "It was just an instinct."

No one can predict how people will act in life-threatening situations, but Rothkopf took initiative and saved a life without thinking twice.

"Charlie helped me get through it; he gave me moral support and kept giving me water to make sure that I did not pass out," Baez said. "And he gave me the shirt that was on my leg and sometimes helped me hold my leg."

Rothkopf was not the only source of assistance to Baez that day.

Proietto, also a student in Lazar's fourth-hour class, had background knowledge of what to do in an emergency situation thanks to her sister, who works as a paramedic. She was able to assist Baez by compressing the gash to slow the bleeding. She relayed advice to Lazar and Rothkopf to help Baez through the trauma as well.

"I didn't know what was really going on," Proietto said. "It was a lot in the moment, and it helped me not pay attention to what was going on. I was just trying to help Ashley calm down."

Similar to Rothkopf, Proietto did not know Baez on a personal level before that day. Proietto and Baez share a mutual friend but had never interacted beyond a greeting in the hallway a few times. Little did Baez know, two people whose names she didn't even know that morning would end up being a major piece in helping her through this tragedy and potentially saving her life.

"Victoria let me rest my leg on her, and she put pressure on my wound when I couldn't do it," Baez said. "She was worried about how I felt the whole time and helped me through it."

Rothkopf and Proietto successfully saved Baez from potentially bleeding out and showed courage, empathy, and responsiveness with the situation they were placed in.

SPEAKING FROM THE HEART

by Tyra Hemans

My name is Tyra Victoria Hemans, and I was born in Plantation, Florida. At age three, I moved to Ghana in Africa with my grandmother. She's a native Ghanaian, and living there was the experience of a lifetime. I went to school there until I moved back to America at age ten. In my eighth-grade summer, I started to be more focused. My mother registered me for Marjory Stoneman Douglas on the first day of the 2014–15 school year. I'd be taking four core classes and three electives. I remember picking Television Production because there were no other classes I really wanted to take other than woodshop, and MSD didn't offer it.

Walking into my first-period class and seeing all those faces was scary. The teacher was super kind and told me to pick any seat I wanted. One girl was really beautiful and her perfume caught my attention. I asked if I could sit by her, and she didn't mind. She asked me what my name was. I told her, "Tyra Hemans. Yours?" "Meadow Pollack," she said. She was my first friend at that school. Never gonna forget.

Six bells later, I was heading to my last class of the day with a smile on my face. I had almost made it through my first day. But when I got to my TV Production class, I had those damn butterflies in my stomach again. It looked like a news station, and I thought that was super cool. I met my teacher, Mr. Eric Garner. He turned out to be one of the nicest teachers I've ever met and made me feel at ease. I knew I had finally found a class I belonged in.

Three years later . . . I'm finally a senior. February 14, a universal day for love. My last Valentine's Day at Douglas will never leave me. It was a normal day. I woke up late, picked up my friends, and went to school. I saw everyone in red, hugs and kisses all around. We were all feeling the love in the air. Like the rest of my friends, I couldn't wait to be with my boyfriend after school. By one o'clock I was on my way to class. I was debating whether I wanted to skip it and go to either Garner (TV class) or Jacobson (eleventh-grade reading teacher). Thank God I didn't go to Jacobson. Her classroom is located on the third floor of the Freshman Building. I decided not to skip and be a good student, so I went to my fourth-period class. I was so sleepy, I put my head on my desk. My stomach was telling me something wasn't right. I asked to use the bathroom. I ran out of class and kept walking because I didn't know where to go. I just knew something was happening.

I ended up in Garner's class, where I'd always felt safe. I walked in the back room and started talking to some friends in there. It was a quick conversation. I stayed in Garner's room a total of three minutes, then I left the room saying, "Bye, Garner, love you." He responded, "Love ya back, kid."

I just felt like I had to keep moving. My next stop was the Freshman Building. As I got closer, I felt something in my gut—I knew the wave of worry was coming from there. I walked to the bathroom—it was locked. I sensed something was really wrong, so I left the building. When I got outside, I heard a big boom. Still, I didn't think it was the sound of a bullet—since I was near the culinary room, maybe the noise was coming from there. So I decided to walk back to class because I needed to get my stuff.

In less than thirty seconds, the fire alarm went off. I panicked and started running. I didn't know what was happening because we had had a drill earlier that day (that was the last time I saw my friend Meadow), and this didn't seem like a drill.

I was lucky that I made it to class with enough time to grab my stuff and call my mom because the teacher told us there was a Code Red. I knew by then that something was really wrong. My class left the building and was evacuated nearby to Walmart. I was with my classmate Devin, who was on crutches at the time. Running was hard for him, so I encouraged him to go faster.

As we were running to Walmart, Devin and I both stopped when we saw a crying lady coming our way. She just dropped to the ground, crying and talking in a different language. I looked into the woman's eyes and could tell she was a mother. I couldn't help her because she couldn't speak English. I tried to read her phone and see what language she spoke and was able to narrow it down to Spanish or Portuguese. I called out to see if anyone spoke those languages. No one answered; everyone was running. She got up and started running again, this time heading back toward the school. I couldn't follow her, so Devin and I kept running.

Devin and I made it to Walmart. We knew by then it had to be a real shooting, but we didn't know the details. We had to ask ourselves if a shooting really just happened and played it over and over in our heads. I started to see faces of friends I recognized. I must have been in a daze because my friend Taryn literally snatched me by my braids into her dad's car, and all she could say was Ariel—one of my dear friends I hang out with day in and day out—was in the Freshman Building, where the shooting took place.

We didn't know all the facts. I began to panic. I went from not really focusing on what was happening straight to full-on heart attack. I started to text every group chat, calling everyone. We got to Taryn's neighborhood, hopped out of the car, and ran to her living room to turn on the TV—just to see that this had become my reality. My school.

I was still in disbelief. On TV we were seeing people leaving the Freshman Building. I was staring at the screen, seeing which of my friends were still alive. They showed on the screen that seven people were confirmed dead. Every hour, that number went up.

Once I had my car back, I saw my cousin and gave him a ride. Ten minutes later my friend Liz called me, asking if I had heard from Meadow. My heart dropped. I instantly hung up the phone and dialed Meadow's phone number multiple times. I texted her multiple times. She did not respond. Later my cousin Bianca, who was on the third floor of the Freshman Building, called me to say that she was fine, but a friend of mine was on the floor dead. To this day, I will never get that phone call out of my head. She told me another close friend, Guac (Joaquin Oliver), was dead. I dropped the phone. I didn't cry. I couldn't cry. I was in shock. Later, on the news, the number of seven turned to ten . . . fifteen by midnight. By morning, seventeen people from my school had been pronounced dead, and thirty-two people were injured. That morning, I was told that three people I loved were dead: Joaquin (Guac) Oliver, Meadow Pollack, and Coach Aaron Feis. Later in the day I heard about Helena Ramsay, a classmate of mine. I had just seen her at first-period sociology class that day. It didn't seem real.

I was in the shower when I broke down. I cried for hours. The water pierced my body and I just let it. I sat there saying "seventeen," knowing they were angels. When I was able to come to life again, I decided that I couldn't weep anymore. I just couldn't. I had to do something instead. I went to Walgreens, bought posters, and printed two pictures, Guac's and Feis's. I don't know why—I just did it. I was letting my broken heart lead this journey.

I had completed Guac and Feis's poster only to be hit with tears again. I was happy I was home alone. I couldn't have anyone see me this way. I was in shambles. While I was making my second poster, the rage began. I could only see red. The red reminded me of the blood that stained the halls. The red reminded me of the rage that monster must have felt when he decided it was time for my friends to die. I was ready to go back over to school. I knew that I was not a violent child. I was not taking that route. But I knew I had to change this politically.

As the school came into view, it was time to face my demon. I was the only student there. It had become a crime scene, blocked off so no one could get close. And where there is a crime scene, there are news vans and reporters. Every news outlet you could think of was out there. I just kept walking, only to be stopped by the cops. I had to stop at the overpass. That's when I just lifted my posters. I was crying. I didn't care. I had to show the world what an AR-15 rifle did to me. It killed my friends. Murdered and slaughtered them. A man came into my school and hunted my classmates. I was under the overpass for three or four hours holding my posters. I knew I wanted to go to the vigil at Pine Trails Park, but I couldn't leave.

Later my friend Tyra B. told me more about Meadow. She was shot nine times. It was like they had just put the cherry on the top of my insanity. I lost it. I was on the floor wailing "Meadow, Meadow, Meadow." An AR-15 killed my friend, my best friend, my first friend, at school. I called my mother and just cried, saying "Meadow, Meadow." I couldn't keep it together and needed to stay busy, so I left and stopped at a craft store, then a drugstore. Printing out Meadow's picture was probably the hardest thing I could have ever done after hearing such tragic news. I went home and finished her poster. I made it to Pine Trails Park for the vigil in tears. I felt so bad. What used to be a community park was now a memorial site.

A few days later, I went on a bus trip with other MSD students to Tallahassee to meet our state leaders and senators. FSU let us stay in their dorms for the night, and the next day our activism began. I was ready for them. I didn't write any speeches or essays. I spoke from the heart, which was filled with fury because

I believed the inaction of these politicians killed my friends. Their laws allowed gun violence and mental health issues to be swept under the rug. While I was speaking to Governor Rick Scott and members of the Florida senate, I felt pure raw emotion. I don't think they will forget me. I said, "Look into my eyes. I lost three people to the shooting." I said their names: Meadow Pollack. Guac [Joaquin Oliver]. Coach Feis. "Look me in the eyes and tell me right now that because of guns, I can't walk these streets again. . . . I can't walk my hallways [at school] because I am always reminded of an AR-15 military rifle assault weapon shooting my hallways. . . . How would you feel knowing that your kid going to school on Valentine's Day is never going to come home, 'cause the last ten minutes of school was their last ten minutes of life? Look me in the eyes when I am saying my friends are gone but they will never be forgotten because . . . me and my peers at MSD, we will not stop fighting." They didn't answer me—they just said they wanted to make sure everyone had a chance to speak—but that didn't stop me.

Two weeks later we had to return to school. I hated everything about it. I told myself that I was doing it for our lost friends. Around this time David Hogg told me about the March For Our Lives event in D.C. I thought, This is it. I can tell everyone exactly what we need. So I took the bus to the march in D.C.

The night before the march, Guac appeared in my dreams. That's when I knew it was really something I had to do. I wasn't on the list of speakers, but I had to speak. The day of the march, I saw a former classmate in a blocked-off area. I got her attention, then saw my former English teacher, Mrs. Falkowski. She gave me her last press pass, which is how I got onstage. By the end, my good friend Emma González gave me the mic, and it was my time to speak. I panicked. Did I belong up there? I wasn't an AP student like the others. I'm an immigrant who, before I could drive, was bused into Parkland, a top school district. I looked down and saw my TV teacher, Eric Garner. He motioned to his heart, and I could see him mouthing, "Say what's in your heart." I thought, Tell the truth. I spoke from the heart and the crowd responded. I could tell they agreed. We need change in America.

I did not stop there. I will not let the world forget my friends, or any other victim of gun violence. I followed up with David at the beginning of the summer because I wanted to do more activist work. He told me about the March For Our Lives Road to Change tour, and I went with them to Chicago. In Chicago, I worked with other gun violence activists, some of the smartest people I have ever met. They are humble and they know the value of a person. For that, I thank them. They will save our country.

My mother, Nadine, once told me that if people try to stop you from leading or speaking, you just have to push twice as hard. She is the reason I am on a mission to end gun violence. My mother taught me that I am strong and cannot be silenced.

SELF-CARE: MANAGING YOUR TRAUMA

by Leni Steinhardt

Regardless of a student's or teacher's experience on February 14 or their proximity to the shooting, what occurred on that day left a haunting grip on the entire Marjory Stoneman Douglas High School community. Even if we escaped school that day, many of us have found it difficult to escape the challenging and scary new world around us. Some people now suffer from PTSD or anxiety, which is hard to handle without the proper self-care and help.

One thing that I've certainly learned is that whether it is a cognitive, physical, or behavioral reaction to trauma, it is important to manage your emotions and seek the help of a parent, friend, teacher, or therapist. This is not a cookie-cutter situation and is more of an experiment trying to find what works best for you and what can get you through your everyday roller coaster of emotions.

Likewise, there is no wrong or right way to respond to these emotions. However, it is important to recognize the many people in your life who are ready to help you recover and the many resources available to help you get there, which I never fully realized until after the shooting.

One thing that especially helped me after the shooting was seeking therapy. My parents knew that they could never understand the pain that my brother and I felt that day or our many emotions following it. Instead, they thought that therapy would allow us a platform to discuss openly how we were feeling.

Not only did seeing a therapist make me realize my biggest strengths, it helped me realize all the love surrounding me. My therapist checked up on me as well after our sessions and made sure I was doing okay. These therapists wanted to help me and sought out ways for me to stay positive during the toughest days of my life, and I am forever thankful for that. It is important to acknowledge the love in the world and not the hate, especially after a large-scale tragedy.

I also searched for other ways to help manage my many emotions. At home, I tried to decrease my exposure to the media. Reliving the events of that day by reading articles or watching news segments on television triggered inner emotions that I had tried to suppress. These triggers put me in a dark place that prompted unwanted memories. Now there are many triggers in my life that I have to deal with every day—car alarms, loud bangs, crowded spaces, dark rooms, and the sound of emergency vehicles all take me back to that day.

Some ways to avoid these triggers are to be cautious, try my best to focus on hobbies, and find time to have fun and do leisure activities. I am on the girls' varsity golf team, and in the weeks following the shooting, I was frequently on the golf range. It was a quiet place that allowed me to focus more on my strengths than on my weaknesses. Also, by spending time with friends and family, I was able to surround myself with positive thoughts and people.

Just as important, I found that small things like sleeping and exercising helped me maintain a healthy lifestyle. After the shooting, I lacked the motivation to leave my house. Just jogging around my neighborhood gave me the opportunity to clear my head and have a healthy amount of me time. Another thing that I did, which coincided with jogging, was establishing a routine. A routine enabled me to be more productive and minimized the number of drastic changes in my life.

It was also important for me to set goals for myself. Whether they were small, like sleeping a whole eight hours, or big, like getting straight As in school, I felt that by setting these goals I could take more control over my life and give myself a mission to focus on.

I also highly recommend journaling to anyone going through a difficult time. After the shooting, I found it difficult to talk about my emotions. There was just no way to explain how I felt. Journaling helped me reflect on my emotions and make sense of what I was feeling. One idea that a friend had suggested to me was to write down five good things that happened each day. By doing this, I took more notice of my surroundings and my interactions with the people in my life. This helped me appreciate all the good that is in my life and the simple things that make it so great.

It was also important to admit that I needed help. I am a strongheaded person, and I feel the need to handle my own challenges without involving other people. However, when it comes to a traumatic experience like this, I knew that I would not have been able to deal with these feelings on my own, and that the first step in getting help was admitting that I needed it.

Part of my healing was learning that it is important to allow myself to cry. Bottling up my emotions only kept all my frightening and depressing feelings inside, preventing me from feeling happy. Without crying I was a ticking time bomb full of emotions. Healing through crying proved to be my release, not my defeat.

Dealing with an extremely traumatic event at such a young age puts a heavy weight on everyone's shoulders. Though my life has changed since the events at my school, I feel more hopeful that through self-care I have better managed my new emotions. There is no manual to teach you how to cope with any trauma, and each day is a new battle and learning experience. Just remember, you are not alone. Whether you are dealing with a major trauma like the shooting at my school, or an everyday challenge or rough patch in your life, remember that we all could use help at times, and there are many ways to get it—once you admit that you need it.

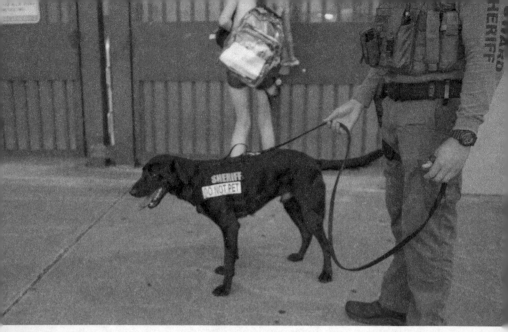

DAY TO DAY
What Will the Future Bring?

by Daniel Cuervo

From day to day, we do the same. For four long (short?) years we hold the same but ever-evolving ambitions that we hope eventually develop into our futures. Freshman year we begin a new chapter of our lives that represents opportunity and potential. In our sophomore year, we settle in. We start to consider the path of knowledge we will choose to pursue to prepare us for our future careers. Junior year is the climax, when we start deciding where we want to go and what we wish to do. We worry about what our SAT scores will be and acquiring the credits for our AP courses that will assist us along the road to our next chapters. Our senior year is the final page of this chapter, where we complete our requirements and receive our final transcripts before transitioning to our next chapters.

Change in life is imminent, and we are now prepared for its initiation. However, the unimaginable occurred, a concept of high school life we were not prepared for. Our words, our pages, our series—violated. What we'd meant to be our proud novels now became tattered tragedies. Over three thousand stories torn to ruin. Seventeen burned. All our books—our lives on hiatus. Days are long, and hours so short, as we remember what was lost and who. . . . Life has never seemed so foreign. We now live day to day, sitting, fearing, and mourning.

Life seems forever changed after an experience such as this. Frequent phone calls and messages from news reporters asking questions we were asking ourselves. Cameras surrounding us as we held each other as if we would never get another chance to. Our school's name known across the nation, and all eyes and ears directed on us. We were the topic that was being discussed in every corner of the country. We were the story that piqued present interest. Day to day we witnessed the advance of media and journalism firsthand. February was the most intense. When we found the power to leave the shelter of our homes, it was impossible not to see at least four news vans and at least one helicopter. Reporters clawing through each other for the opportunity to get an interview. When March came around, we began the effort to be heard. We were sick and tired of being sick and tired. Quickly the pity and sentiment turned into hate. Half of America now glared at us. Although we've had an immense amount of support, the feeling of having thousands of people pushing against you in a time of hardship was so overwhelming. More opportunity and cameras were presented. Come April, interest withered, as any news story does. Day to day, we watch change at our school: new ID requirements, clear backpacks, new policies and points of entry on campus. All no longer newsworthy in the eyes of the media. It is now May 16, 7:43 p.m., and news of our school becomes very scarce.

With all the questions we've been asked these past months, the one that has yet to be asked of me and my fellow classmates is the one I've been asking myself since that day: "What of the future?" I don't mean what will become of the rules of school safety or who will be elected to pass new gun laws. I'm talking about the future that my peers and I will face when we leave our school. How will we handle this trauma when we're on our own? This fear that the person next to me may be the end of me? The thought of us progressing when our dear friends never got the chance? How can we live when our lives have changed so drastically? Hundreds of students are now leaving Marjory Stoneman Douglas High School with the memory of a face against a gun barrel. Yet it seems as though the media is not interested in what we do afterward. That it was not our lives that were the story, but the tragedy itself. What of our future?

Day to day, we will remember what we lost and will share the endless ambition of getting back what we had. Day to day, we will remember who we lost so that we may continue to reach for our goals to honor those who shared our dreams. Day to day, we will fight the demon we all now share so that no others will be possessed by it ever again.

THE ROAD TO CHANGE

by David Hogg

It is hard to believe that all of this has happened in the same calendar year. From our lives as normal high school students, to activists born of tragedy, to caricatures of the gun lobby and many of their supporters, 2018 has changed our lives forever and set us on a path to effect sane gun laws for America once and for all.

The shooting at our school also sent me and my friends on a journey into the heart of our country, and on this journey we have discovered that Americans are more divided than ever before. These divisions are exploited and encouraged by those at the top, the people we once called "leaders," who are supposed to make our democracy function, smooth over our differences, and lead us toward solutions to our problems. Instead, our "leaders" too often have us at each other's throats and encourage us to think the very worst of each other, which only hardens positions and hearts, reinforces biases, and closes minds and ears. This is no way for adults to behave, and no way to solve problems, much less run a country.

This is the world that we are trying to change. These polarized politics existed before February 14, 2018, and it is obviously not just about gun violence and not just about the Second Amendment. There are deep cultural chasms in the country—regional, religious, economic, political—and all of us find it too easy to go to our corners with our tribes when a serious and divisive issue comes up. The mistrust in this country is just intolerable. This politics of dehumanization dehumanizes us all and makes it easier to be perpetual, intractable enemies, forever unable to even talk to each other. But the dirty little secret is that this just plays into the hands of the powerful lobbies, because that way the status quo prevails, kids remain at risk in their schools and communities, and nothing ever changes for the better. It is only by looking each other in the eye and speaking from the heart that we will have a chance to understand each other, respectfully explain ourselves to each other, *rehumanize* each other, and defeat the deeply troubling vision that we have discovered of an America forever reduced to warring camps. I believe in my heart that very few people want to live like that.

As I begin to write this—from Bismarck, North Dakota—the March For Our Lives group is preparing for a rally in our Road to Change tour. This evening, we are projected to have a good group at the rally—here to talk about sensible solutions to our undeniable problem of gun violence, register to vote, maybe volunteer—but that crowd is also expected to be dwarfed by protesters. And one task that we could not have counted on having to do when we first got started in this effort is having to clear up so much slander that has been spread about us—in my case, especially, the nonsense that I was not at Marjory Stoneman Douglas High School that day, that I was not even a student there, that I am a professional "crisis actor," that I am ABC news anchor David Muir, that I am a shape-shifting lizard, etc., etc., etc.

These are the times in which we live.

When my friends and I survived the murder of seventeen of our schoolmates, we felt compelled to enter into an arena that was alien to us—politics—with the goal of being engaged citizens and appealing for commonsense laws to change the circumstances that made our friends' murders possible. I am not sure what we thought the response of the world would be, but to see a fictional villainous version of yourself emerge from internet trolls and ideologues and Alex Jones, well, that certainly is something I never imagined. And because there have been so many outrageous and untrue things written and said about us, the protesters we meet often expect the absolute worst at first. They are angry and worked up, calling us "gun grabbers" and things like that. It takes a long time to undo that misconception, to show a human face, to persuade people who have been conditioned to hate us and our views that we aren't the bogeymen that they have been told we are.

All of this takes patience and kindness, qualities that sometimes honestly are in short supply. But it is the only thing to do, because, to quote that wise saying, you've got to be the change you wish to see in the world. And screaming and yelling and calling people stupid is not only rude, but it will also accomplish precisely nothing. When you are going to new towns and asking to be heard, the most important thing you can do is listen to the people who live there. Hear their stories, learn their perspectives, find connections, because they are there. Before we are Democrats or Republicans, red or blue, we are all human. We all have experienced loss and pain and joy. We all have families and friends and hometowns. As John Kennedy once said when talking about resolving the differences of a different time, "We all inhabit this small planet. We all breathe the same air. We all cherish our children's future. And we are all mortal."

Please do not misunderstand me—our goals to make America safer do involve political solutions, and politics asks you to make choices. One candidate over another, one value judgment over another, one solution over another. Democracy is by nature about choices, and choices can be divisive. We will fight for our goals, we will not relent, and we will not give up. But we in March For Our Lives have learned through this baptism by fire in 2018 that the world is not improved by vilifying each other. In addition to being childish and wrong, vilification is also inefficient, in that it is a terrible way to achieve your desired result, and so we'll leave the vilification to other people as we set about in good faith to convert our pain and loss into action that changes our world for the better.

We will continue to talk to any audience in any town anywhere to convey the simple, strong message that commonsense legislation does not mean taking your guns away—it means saving lives. And we will continue to work during the coming election and all the elections to follow to support moral candidates who will value lives over lobbyist dollars and common sense over ideology. And we will continue to describe things as they are, and to tell the truth—about who is and who is not a captive of the gun lobby, which seeks to keep us afraid and keep us divided. We will continue to use the technologies available to us to address the whole world, even as we cherish meeting and talking to new individuals in town after town, whether we agree or disagree.

The anger we felt after February 14 may have been our initial adrenaline in this marathon, but love and compassion will be what keep us going. We won't reach everybody—some people will have no interest in hearing our perspective, and that's okay. But we will reach a lot more people than have been reached in the past, when all sides have been stuck in their well-dug trenches, hurling rocks and mortars at each other.

And in this spirit, sure enough, around Independence Day, our Road to Change tour found itself in Dallas, Texas, a proud place of independent-minded people who like to openly carry their weapons in public places, but who also live in a state where a majority—51 percent—favor more commonsense gun laws. And even more Texans than that favor universal background checks. *In Texas.* As we were doing everywhere, we were in Dallas to talk and to listen. As several of us stepped outside the venue where our rally was taking place to meet the protesters who had assembled there, an armed man asked me why I wanted to take his gun away. I told him that I didn't, and that members of my family owned guns. A larger group gathered around, both people with guns and people without, and ninety minutes later, after a sometimes contentious, sometimes very emotional conversation, that man thanked us for helping him understand why we are doing what we are doing. It was as if he had never experienced an honest exchange of ideas before. It was as if he had never been accorded that level of respect for his thoughts. We thanked the man in return.

In the days after that encounter, a few stories appeared in the press. One headline read: "Parkland students and gun owners got into a heated debate that ended in tears and hugs."

Of all the headlines in this terribly sad and wondrous year, that headline just might be my favorite.

Onward.

INDEPENDENT STUDENT-RUN NEWSROOMS

An Imperative for High Schools Nationwide

by Melissa Falkowski

The *Eagle Eye* is an award-winning newsmagazine and has been recognized both locally and nationally for its excellence.

Despite our award-winning history, the *Eagle Eye* staff is always seeking to improve. We are working on improving the multimedia reporting on our website and looking for new in-depth stories to write about in our print newsmagazine. The *Eagle Eye*'s mission remains the same—to give students a voice in their school community.

There are many compelling reasons to strive for a thriving media program in every high school. Student newsrooms are the ultimate exercise in project-based learning. Students work all year to produce physical newspapers to be distributed within the school community. Students learn invaluable skills: communication, teamwork, peer collaboration, analytical thought, leadership, time management, meeting deadlines, clear writing, social media planning, marketing, and advertising sales. School media programs engage in twenty-first-century journalism, using industry-standard software tools like Adobe InDesign, Photoshop, and Final Cut Pro. Student journalists manage multiple social media accounts. All of these experiences prepare them for their future in the digital workplace. What employer wouldn't want employees with these skills?

It is also important that these programs are student-driven and free of administrative censorship. Ten states protect student journalists from school administrators who would seek to censor them. The Student Press Law Center, a nonprofit organization that provides the nation's only legal assistance exclusively to high school journalists, has been working to pass New Voices legislation in many states to expand First Amendment protections for student journalists. Florida does not provide protection to student journalists through statewide legislation, but there are individual school districts, like Miami-Dade County Public Schools, that do. Unfortunately, Broward County Public Schools do not. Student journalists and publication advisers alike are looking forward to when our state legislature will take up and pass New Voices here in Florida or our school board will prohibit administrators from censoring student journalists as part of the student code of conduct, as Miami-Dade has.

In the meantime, MSD's *Eagle Eye* is operated as a student-run newsroom. Student reporters and editors drive the content and editorial decisions for our print and online publications. As their adviser, I don't tell them what stories to write and publish—my responsibility is to guide them and make sure that they are reporting responsibly, but also to encourage them to take up the hard-hitting stories that they want to explore. I groan and jokingly ask them why they want to get me fired when they pitch controversial stories in our planning sessions, because I know we will deal with complaints and I will end up having to defend them. But I also tell them that if they are making the grown-ups in the room uncomfortable, then they are probably doing something right.

There have been several stories over my last three years advising the *Eagle Eye* that have come under scrutiny. We are fortunate to have an administration and a principal who support the students' First Amendment right to free expression. Our principal, Ty Thompson, has both commended them on their stories and vigorously defended them to parents and community members who have complained about specific stories.

Student publications are often thought of as public relations tools for the school—a place for only positive or happy news. However, that is not the purpose of student publications, which explore student issues, expose school-related problems, and serve as an opportunity for students to question their "government," which in this case is school administration or leadership in the school district. Teaching students to think critically and question decisions from their "government" forms the groundwork for them to apply those skills later within American society. As the

Washington Post's slogan says, "Democracy dies in the darkness." Teaching students to report only happy, positive news does not prepare them to go out and defend our democracy as citizens.

Research by the Newspaper Association of America Foundation demonstrates that students who participate in high school journalism programs get better grades, score higher on the ACT, and even earn higher grades as college freshmen. But I don't need those figures. I have seen firsthand how journalism programs have helped my students excel, with top grades and high test scores. I've also seen how it has empowered this generation of journalists to use their voices, training, and experience in a way that captures national attention and facilitates change. That is why I hope our staff at MSD continues to teach this generation of children. I'm committed to my job as a teacher, empowering students to use their voices and their tools—as journalists, students, and citizens of the world—to uncover and report the truth.

HONORING OUR FALLEN EAGLES

MSD's newspaper, the *Eagle Eye,* produced a special Memorial Issue in honor of the seventeen students and faculty who lost their lives on February 14, 2018. Through interviews with each student's friends and families, along with their own personal insights, the student reporters put together seventeen in-depth profiles. You can access the full Memorial Issue here: *issuu.com/melissafalkowski4/*

Photo by Melissa Falkowski

For more reporting from the *Eagle Eye,* visit us at:
Website: eagleeye.news
Twitter: @EagleEyeMSD
Instagram: @HumansofMSD

MSD's Broadcast Journalism class, WMSD-TV, produced the *#MSDStrong* documentary, an homage to the school community and the national reaction to the shooting. The documentary includes interviews with the school's burgeoning student activists, along with teachers and alumni from as far as New York, California, and Hawaii: *tinyurl.com/yd2ow363*

"THERE IS ALWAYS THE NEED TO CARRY ON."
- Marjory Stoneman Douglas (1890-1998)

Photo by Eric Garner

MSD MEDIA AWARDS AND ACCOLADES

All of our school media programs—including the *Eagle Eye* newspaper, *Aerie* yearbook, WMSD-TV, and *Artifex* literary magazine—are award-winning, both in the state of Florida and on the national level.

THE *EAGLE EYE*'S AWARDS

The National Scholastic Press Association/Journalism Education Association

- Awarded with a Pacemaker, the Pulitzer Prize of student journalism, in November 2017. Pacemaker winners represent the top 1 percent of student newspapers in the nation.
- Awarded the very first Courage and Commitment Award for "the presence of mind and clarity of purpose to think like journalists during and in the immediate aftermath of the most traumatic incident of their lives."
- Awarded the Special Recognition Impact Award for coverage of the shooting and its aftermath, and creating a national debate on gun control in spring 2018

The Columbia Scholastic Press Association

- Awarded the *Eagle Eye* with a Gold Crown in March 2018, the Pacemaker equivalent for their organization, based on reporting from the 2016–17 school year

Florida Scholastic Press Association
- Rated All-Florida, their highest rating, for the last three years
- Marjory Stoneman Douglas Award for positive activism through media, spring 2018

The *Sun-Sentinel*'s High School Journalism Awards
- Best High School Newspaper in Broward County, 2016, 2017, 2018
- Best Use of Social Media, 2016, 2017, 2018
- Best Website, 2017, 2018
- Best Layout Design, 2017, 2018
- Best Special Project, 2018
- Adviser of the Year—Melissa Falkowski, 2016, 2018
- Journalist of the Year—Rebecca Schneid, 2018 (inaugural year), sponsored by the Florida Society of Professional Journalists

The Global Center
- Danny Schechter Global Vision Award for Journalism and Activism, 2018

WMSD-TV'S AWARDS

Florida Association for Media in Education
- First Place at Districts for MSD Documentary, 2018
- First Place at Regionals for MSD Documentary, 2018

Florida Scholastic Press Association
- First Place at Districts for Broadcast Commentary, 2017
- First Place at Districts for Live-to-Tape Broadcast, 2015, 2016

- Marjory Stoneman Douglas Award for positive activism through media, spring 2018

Student Television Network
- First Place at Nationals for Movie Trailer, 2017
- Third Place at Nationals for Spot News Feature, 2016
- First Place at Nationals for Multimedia, 2014

C-SPAN StudentCam
- National Honorable Mention for the video "Target," which focused on gun violence in schools, 2016

Production of a promotional video for the City of Parkland, along with promotionals for each of its recreational areas. This project has been ongoing with the city since 2014.

Members of the *Eagle Eye* staff pose with their awards from *Sun-Sentinel*'s High School Journalism Awards ceremony in April 2018. From left to right, front row: Christy Ma, Nikhita Nookala, Carly Novell, Lauren Newman, Mackenzie Quinn, Richard Doan, Rebecca Schneid, Suzanna Barna. Second row: Melissa Falkowski, Nyan Clarke, Dara Rosen, Taylor Yon, Emma Dowd, Tyler Avron, Einav Cohen, Leni Steinhardt, Brianna Fisher, Delaney Tarr. Third row: Ryan Lofurno, Daniel Pirtle, Kevin Trejos.
Photo by David Schneid

Eric Garner accepts the Marjory Stoneman Douglas Award, which recognizes the courage of student journalists at MSD, during the Florida Scholastic Press Association State Convention in April 2018. From left to right: Valentina Sawan, Mia Yara, Ryan Senatore, Chris Cahill, Luke Tiplea, Daniel Sarig, Alyssa Marrero, Gilon Kravatsky, Josh Riemer, Sam Grizelj, Eric Garner, Navid Rafiee, Arianna Casamento, Emily Sucher, Manolo Alvarez, Taylor Freed, Rebecca Leal.
Photo by Brit Taylor

MEET THE CONTRIBUTORS

*Note: All ages reflect the school year the contributor was in on February 14, 2018.

Suzanna Barna (senior) was a first-year staffer for the *Eagle Eye*. Suzanna was a member of the National Honor Society, the Key Club, and various clubs at school. She was also known for hosting a community service program for the senior citizens at Aston Gardens. Suzanna will study civil engineering and business administration at the University of Florida in the fall, and plans to write for the student-run publication the *Alligator*.

Chris Cahill (senior) was a television production and film student for three years. In that time he worked on countless news stories, short films, music videos, and documentaries. He worked as a producer on the *#MSDStrong* documentary, mainly focusing on activism and students' return to school. He plans to attend Florida Atlantic University this fall and continue making short films and documentaries.

Daniel Cuervo (senior) joined WMSD-TV in his freshman year and has participated in competitions sponsored by C-SPAN, Broward Teen News, Florida Scholastic Press Association, and Student Television Network. During his senior year, he was the secretary of TV Club and hopes he contributed to the prosperity of the WMSD-TV program. Daniel aspires to one day combine journalism and health science into a career.

Ryan Deitsch (senior) was a television production and film student for all four years of high school and a newspaper student for one year. Ryan was an integral member of the WMSD-TV team who created a public service announcement that was recognized at the Tribeca Film Festival. He also led competition teams at regional and national TV Production conferences. Ryan is part of the March For Our Lives content team and is taking a gap year to work on registering voters for the midterm elections.

Richard Doan (senior) was a first-year staff writer at the *Eagle Eye*. He earned numerous business awards through DECA competitions at the district, state, and international level. He also served as the president of MSD's Astronomy Club and as an active member of Mu Alpha Theta and the Science National Honor Society. Richard plans to major in business administration at the University of Florida, but hopes to continue his writing career with the school's student publication the *Alligator*.

Melissa Falkowski has been the faculty adviser of the *Eagle Eye* for the last three years. During her fourteen years teaching English and creative writing at MSD, she used to advise the MSD *Aerie* yearbook staff and currently advises the literary magazine, *Artifex*. Once a student journalist herself, Melissa became a teacher to empower students and help them find their voices through journalism. When Melissa is not working, she enjoys spending time with her husband, John; her son, John Thomas; and her daughter, Evangeline.

Brianna Fisher (sophomore) is a first-year staff writer for the *Eagle Eye* newspaper. She was the freshman class president and a sophomore class senator and is an incoming junior class senator. Brianna is also a member of the Math Honor Society, the National English Honor Society, and the National Association of Students Against Gun Violence. She is involved with Dance Marathon, as a morale captain in 2017–18 and the partnership chair on the executive board for 2018–19. Brianna plans to double major in political science and criminology and minor in cognitive psychology in college.

Eric Garner leads the Television Production Academy at MSD, preparing students for the broadcast journalism and film industries. He has been a television production and film instructor for over twenty-five years and has worked at WPTV in West Palm Beach, Florida's News Channel, and WTVJ in Miami/Fort Lauderdale. He also works as a freelancer for independent productions and acts in movies and television. Eric was the executive producer of the *#MSDStrong* documentary, highlighting the activism of the students at MSD after the February 14, 2018, mass shooting.

Zoe Gordon (sophomore) is a first-year staff writer for the *Eagle Eye*. She is also involved in the Math Honor Society, the Key Club, and the National Association of Students Against Gun Violence. In the upcoming school year, she will be a treasurer for the National English Honor Society and a senator for the 2020 class board. Her love for journalism expanded after reporting on the March For Our Lives in D.C. and interviewing people with unique stories. In the future, she hopes to double major in advertising and broadcast communications/journalism.

Augustus Griffith Jr. (junior) is a devout writer from Parkland. He is the secretary of the school's TV Production club, and he recently published his first ebook, *Running in Circles: A Poetry Collection*.

Sam Grizelj (sophomore) has been involved in the TV Production program for the past two years and took on the role of producer in their second class. Sam has created a promotional video for the Parkland Buddy Sports program and is continuing to work on their photography and film skills.

Tyra Hemans (senior) was very active in clubs and programs at MSD. She was in the TV Production program for all four years of high school and was a member of the TV Club. She was on the track and field team and was in the Drama Club. Now she is a proud activist, fighting to help create positive change in the United States.

David Hogg (senior) joined the TV Production program and Debate because he likes arguing and informing people. His pastimes include activism, activism, and more activism. David's favorite thing to do is to create positive and effective change in a world full of pain.

Daniella Infantino (senior) was involved in the TV Production program, where she filmed community and sporting events for three years. She will attend the University of Florida as a double major in political science and criminology and law. Her goal is to become a criminal prosecutor so she can serve justice in her community.

Zakari Kostzer (junior) is the communications director of the TV Production program at Marjory Stoneman Douglas High School. He has been in the program for three years. Most recently he worked as the producer for the *#MSDStrong* documentary and has been a student reporter for such events as March For Our Lives: Parkland, From Broadway With Love: Parkland, and the Feis Bowl.

Christy Ma (senior) was a copy editor of the *Eagle Eye*. During her senior year, she was also the co-president of the MSD chapter of Mu Alpha Theta, recording secretary of the Science National Honor Society, co-treasurer of the National English Honor Society, and a member of the National Honor Society. Although she will attend the University of Florida as a nursing major, Christy is open to journalism as a profession and hopes to be involved in a student publication at the university level.

Lewis Mizen (senior) was a first-year staffer for the *Eagle Eye*. He has served as MSD's Astronomy Club president, secretary of the Politics and Improv clubs, treasurer of TV Production and Rho Kappa, parliamentarian of Lyrical Theory, a member of five honor societies, and a coach in the Parkland recreational soccer league. Lewis's leadership experience allowed him to become an active face of the #NeverAgain movement in the United Kingdom, his home country. Lewis will be studying political science at Florida State University and will also serve as the collegiate representative for Empower the People.

Nikhita Nookala (senior) was a first-year copy editor at the *Eagle Eye*. During her senior year, she held officer positions on the boards of the National English Honor Society, Mu Alpha Theta, and Rho Kappa, and has been a member of the National Honor Society and the Politics Club. Though Nikhita will pursue a major in microbiology at the University of Florida in the fall, she hopes to continue to foster her love for politics and journalism through the various student publications and organizations.

Carly Novell (senior) was an editor for *Eagle Eye*. Carly joined the staff in her junior year after discovering her love for journalism in an elective class. Her passion comes from the power of journalism to give a voice and a platform to those who don't have one. She will continue to find her voice as a reporter at George Washington University in the fall as a journalism major.

Andy Pedroza (senior) participated in the school's TV Production class for three years. He filmed numerous events and flew to Tennessee to attend the national Student Television Network competition. Andy enjoys videography and the art of screenwriting, and he has written numerous scripts that he plans to film in the future.

Josh Riemer (sophomore) is a photographer and videographer. He is an active member of the Parkland community, volunteering and working as a photographer for local businesses. He is also the vice president of the TV Production club at MSD and was named artist of the month at the Parkland Library in January 2018.

Dara Rosen (sophomore) is a first-year staff writer for the *Eagle Eye*. She is also a member of the MSD chapter of the National Association of Students Against Gun Violence. Dara's passion for journalism grew when she and other *Eagle Eye* staff took a trip to New York City, where they toured the *Wall Street Journal,* sat in on a meeting with Rachel Maddow, and collaborated with the *Guardian*. Dara hopes to work for a major publication one day.

Rebecca Schneid (junior) is a second-year staff member of the *Eagle Eye* and served as co-editor-in-chief in the 2017–18 school year. She is also an officer of the Politics Club, the Key Club, and the Spanish Honor Society, and has been a member of the National Honor Society, the National English Honor Society, and the Math Honor Society. While Rebecca has a passion for biology, she has found her true calling in political science and journalism, where she enjoys writing hard-hitting features.

Leni Steinhardt (sophomore) is a first-year staff writer for the *Eagle Eye*. She is a member of Students Demand Action, the National Association of Students Against Gun Violence, and the girls' varsity golf team, and is treasurer of the National English Honor Society. She is also the marketing and publicity chair of

Dance Marathon and will be a morale captain for the 2018 event, is the historian of her local BBYO chapter, and was a freshman class senator. Leni is a two-year recipient of the Underclassman Award for Journalism and Newspaper and hopes to major in journalism and mass communication in college and pursue a career in the field.

Delaney Tarr (senior) was a staff member on the *Eagle Eye* newspaper and the president of the school's TV Production program. Dedicated to both print and broadcast journalism, she worked in front of and behind the camera, anchoring and producing. She has used her journalism skills in her position as project strategist for March For Our Lives. Delaney is taking a gap semester to work on activism through the midterm elections, and she will attend the University of Georgia in the spring to study journalism and communications.

Kevin Trejos (senior) was a staff writer at the *Eagle Eye* newspaper. He was also the 2017–18 president of the MSD Politics Club—dedicated to promoting civic engagement and civil political discourse. He works as a policy strategist for the March For Our Lives organization and cofounded #NeverAgain: Pick Up a Pen, the #NeverAgain movement, and March For Our Lives. At school, he was involved in the Key Club, Rho Kappa, Mu Alpha Theta, the Science National Honor Society, and DECA. Kevin will attend the University of Florida to major in political science.